Career and Technical Student Organizations: Purpose and Possibility

Dale R. Derrickson, Ed.D.

ISBN 978-0-7414-4306-9

Published by:

INFI∞ITY
PUBLISHING.COM

1094 New Dehaven Street, Suite 100
West Conshohocken, PA 19428-2713
Info@buybooksontheweb.com
www.buybooksontheweb.com
Toll-free (877) BUY BOOK
Local Phone (610) 941-9999
Fax (610) 941-9959

Printed in the United States of America
Published January 2013

Dedication

No one is able to attain any measure of success without the instruction, guidance, and coaching of their teachers and mentors. Once teachers assume the dual roles of teacher and Career and Technical Student Organization advisor, they can commence expanding their student relationships in ways that will make the world a much better place for their students and for themselves.

This book is dedicated to all advisors, past, present, and future. When we stand tall, it is because they have lifted us to stand upon their shoulders.

I am indeed fortunate to have been mentored, taught, assisted, and supported by many advisors. Out of all of these wonderful people, three of my advisors are the most significant. The first two advisors are my parents, Roland and Ramona Derrickson. They provided my first solid foundation of support.

The last advisor has been an extremely important advisor. She is my wife, Karen Downey Derrickson. She sustained me through the construction of all of the many rooms and passageways that were engineered upon the parental foundation, including her priceless contributions to the creation of this book.

Fear of failure may be one of the greatest obstacles to striving for success. My most essential advisors eased my own fear of failure; I knew that their acceptance and encouragement would not diminish when I was not completely successful. Consequently, they enhanced my educational experiences with the opportunity to learn from my mistakes in a secure environment.

Table of Contents

Contents

(continued)

Preface

"There is always one moment in childhood when the door opens
and lets the future in."

Graham Greene

One Person's Story

Tim Lawrence, Executive Director of SkillsUSA, once told me a story of how attending a Vocational-Industrial Clubs of America (VICA) state welding contest was a life-altering experience for him. He was a young man from a remote, coal mining area in West Virginia. At the state event, he saw many business and industry professionals who were there to celebrate the technical skills of the students in the state finals. That was impressive to Tim, and he knew that what he and the other students were doing that day must be important. This experience became one of the inspirational factors in his life that motivated him to succeed in his career area after graduation, to develop into a skilled professional, to become a career and technical education teacher, to work on behalf of career education at a state department of education, to join the staff of a national career and technical student organization, and to become the top executive in that organization (VICA, which later became SkillsUSA).

Tim is fortunate to have enjoyed a successful career. Certainly VICA was not the only motivator in his life. Although career and technical education gave him essential skills, it didn't give him *all* of the skills that he used to have a successful career. But when Tim relates his state competition experience and the importance of that day to his future career plans, it is clear that a door opened for him that day which allowed him to see larger possibilities for himself and his future.

Doors to the Future

It could be argued whether or not one or many doors to the future open in a young person's life. That is not the point here; all passageways have merit. To paraphrase America's first teacher in space, Christa McAuliffe, all teachers can touch the future with their students. There are many opportunities to inspire students about the possibilities of their future; Career and Technical Student Organizations (CTSOs) offer some great opportunities that teachers can use to assist their students in reaching out to their future. It is true that good teachers open doors every day for their students, but CTSO doorways are often among the ones through which students actually walk.

Teachers sometimes fail to see all of the wonderful impact that career and technical student organizations (CTSOs) can have on their students. This is no surprise; good teachers are very busy people. Sometimes they are so busy preparing the soil, planting the roses, fertilizing the roses, pulling the weeds, trimming the rose bushes, protecting the roses, preparing the roses, and harvesting the roses that they don't have enough time to enjoy smelling the roses. Furthermore, when they do smell the roses, they may not have time to bask in the aroma; they are often lucky if they get enough time to take a quick sniff before the next issue or effort prods them on their way. In spite of this, CTSOs can and many times do have a wonderful impact on students.

Impact and Application

One quick measure of the impact on students occurs when teachers and/or other advisors ask former students to come back to assist with or judge a contest. These former students are often very happy to return. They enjoy participating at a higher level in something that they believe is worthwhile. Many will mention that they want to "give back" to an organization that gave so much to them. Many feel honored that they are considered important enough to be asked to participate. Their willingness and enthusiasm show that they received the proper application of their career and technical student organization when they were students.

To achieve a proper application, the benefits of participation should not be offered only to those students who are able to finish at the top. The former students who are enthusiastic about returning to offer some form of assistance to their career and technical student organization shouldn't just be the ones who won a medal. If correctly applied, the honor and praise that they received from participating can be more motivational than a medal. If the ideals and goals of the organization are fully presented, belonging to such an organization can be highly inspirational. If there is a high level of participation from business and industry personnel, their presence can provide support and bring prestige to the students' participation.

What sort of medal did Tim Lawrence win at his state conference? What type of medal did it take to inspire his level of career success? He didn't win a gold medal or a silver medal. He didn't win a bronze medal, either. In fact, he didn't win *any* medal at his VICA state competition. Because Tim had a good role model in his instructor and because he had a positive experience at the state conference, a medal was not needed to get him excited about learning and about his future. It seems that these adults had a good understanding of how the activities of that CTSO could motivate CTE students. A good understanding of the purpose of any CTSO can frame the doorway to the possibilities of a student's future. Thanks to the inspiration of his teacher, Tim did not have to win a medal to have a positive CTSO experience. A medal was not the key to his future success. Thanks to the wisdom and guidance of his teacher and advisor, the door to his future was already unlocked.

Dale R. Derrickson, Ed.D.

Introduction

"All styles are good except the tedious kind."

Voltaire

Distinct, But Similar

The rich diversity of career and technical student organizations follows the rich diversity of career and technical education. Individual supporters of career and technical education may have their individual preference for a specific area or category of areas; however, they should also support career and technical education as a whole. The variations of this type of education have many common methods, goals, and outcomes, as well as their own distinguishing characteristics. To not support the whole of career and technical education would serve to undermine the support of any one specific part.

This text will explore the similarities of purpose and variances of style of the many career and technical student organizations. While explaining their differences is necessary at times, it does not mean that an attempt is being made to rate these organizations through their differences. There are many different ways to accomplish wonderful things for career and technical students. Understanding differences should lead to education rather than discourse.

Career and technical education (CTE) exists at both the secondary and post-secondary level. As a result, CTSOs also exist at both the secondary and post-secondary level. The author intends to use this text for teachers at the secondary level; therefore, the main focus of this text will be on secondary CTSOs.

CTSO List

Throughout this text, the reader will find both the full and abbreviated versions of high school Career and Technical Student Organizations' names at times. The organizations are:

Business Professionals of America (BPA) This organization serves Business Education students.

DECA, An Association of Marketing Students
(Previously DECA represented Distributive Education Clubs of America) This organization serves Marketing students.

Family, Career, and Community Leaders of America (FCCLA) (Previously known as FHA, which was Future Homemakers of America.) This organization serves Family and Consumer Science students.

<u>FFA</u> (Previously Future Farmers of America, now simply FFA) This organization serves Agriscience students.

<u>Future Business Leaders of America (FBLA)</u> This is another organization that serves Business Education students.

<u>Health Occupations Students of America (HOSA)</u> This organization serves Health Occupations Education students.

<u>SkillsUSA</u> (Formerly known as VICA) This organization serves Skilled and Technical Sciences (STS) students (formerly known as Trade and Industrial).

<u>Technology Student Association (TSA)</u> This organization serves Technology Education students.

The reader may have a preference for one of these organizations over all others. This may result from inexperience or experience. There is nothing wrong with having a preference, but one important concept should be understood. These are all great organizations. The intents and purposes of these organizations have vast similarities. The canons of the first of these organizations served to inspire the tenets of later organizations. The biggest difference in these organizations is the career pathways of the students that they serve.

Current Terminology

Another discussion item concerns whether to use the term "vocational" or "career and technical". Vocational is the earlier term used for this specific type of education. This word is still found in many State laws, reflecting the time when these laws were written. The name is still used by some organizations and in some regulations.

The evolution of this name follows the change in name of the American Vocational Association (AVA) in 1999 to the Association for Career and Technical Education (ACTE) through its first use in federal legislation in the Carl D. Perkins Career and Technical Education Act of 2006.

The most important consideration is what the name represents. It is important that a systematic effort of continuous improvement must occur in career and technical education for it to remain a vital component of education. It is also important that we not lose sight of the origins and purposes of vocational education. While the original "vocations" may have added newly developed "career" opportunities, community support and funding for the purpose of career and technical education is often based upon the founding mission.

Both terms will be used in this text. While it may be more fashionable to use the up-to-date "career and technical", references to historical documents and/or occurrences may reflect the word used at the time: "vocational". Readers who prefer the newer "career and technical" name should not take offense when the term "vocational" is used, especially when it is used in an historical context.

Consistency of Support

The need to support all career and technical student organizations was stressed at the beginning of this introduction. While they have different styles, they exist for similar purposes. If supporters of one type of career and technical education cannot support all types, then they must fail to recognize the similarities of these types of organizations. Supporters with a preference for one type of CTSO should not worry about another organization soaking up all of the business community's support. There is usually more than enough support to sustain all of these organizations.

The need to support career and technical students will also be stressed throughout this text, regardless of the individual style or focus of the CTSO. All of this backing is insignificant if career and technical education is not valued by the reader. Chapter One will briefly explore some of the positive attributes of career and technical education. Without a solid foundation of agreement concerning the potential benefits of career and technical education, structures of different styles of this type of education will not be able to stand.

Career and Technical Education (CTE)

CTSOs are not an extracurricular effort for CTE. CTSO activities are co-curricular activities that are a critical component of CTE. While it may occasionally be necessary to separate CTSOs to delve into the specifics of each, it is impossible to separate them in theory. Consequently, they will often be discussed together. Their foundations and inevitabilities will often coincide. If the reader finds a few pages where CTE is discussed without mentioning CTSOs, the intention is that CTSOs are still connected. While CTE may be the equivalent of automotive transport for students' career journeys, CTSOs can provide high-octane fuel to help propel this journey.

Administrative Support

It is hoped that administrators who read this text will be motivated to increase their support of CTSOs, partly due to state and federal mandates, but mostly due to the purpose of these organizations and the possibilities that they present for CTE student success. Teachers who lack administrative support should not shrink from CTSO activities; the activities may be able to garner more administrative support if administrators are able to see them in action.

Whatever the level of administrative support that can be availed, teacher-advisors should come to understand that the most important aspects of CTSO activities take place at the local level. More students can be positively affected at the local level than at the national or state level, and numerous CTSO resources exist to assist teachers if they choose to incorporate these benefits into their CTE program.

Chapter One

Benefits of Career
and Technical Education

"Goodness does not consist in greatness, but greatness in goodness."

Athenaeus

Minority Opinion

CTE teachers often find themselves as the minority of the education staff in their schools. They may find that their views on the benefits of CTE are not always congruent with popular opinions. In spite of this disharmony, as educators, they must strive to enlighten other education staff and their public regarding the positive aspects of their subject matter and all CTE aspects. When CTE is criticized, CTE educators must put the facts in context and accent the positive impact that CTE can have on students' futures.

Allocating Resources

Career and technical education is often in competition for resources with other aspects of a student's education. Art education, core academics education, music education, world language education, remedial education, sports, and even student-based social and health services - all of these facets of education need resources to fulfill their mandates for student education.

One of these resources is money. It takes more money to build and maintain specialized CTE facilities. CTE laboratories usually require more space than academic classrooms. It also takes money to provide the materials that must be expended to teach CTE students in these specialized facilities. What has happened to financial support? States and local municipalities provide CTE support at differing levels, but this support is buttressed with federal financial assistance distributed by the Office of Vocational and Adult Education (OVAE) at the U.S. Department of Education. From federal fiscal year 1990 to fiscal year 2000, overall federal support for all education programs (including academic and CTE) increased by 58.3% as measured in constant FY2000 dollars. During that same decade and using the same measure, federal support for CTE high school and adult education decreased by 6.3% as measured in constant FY2000 dollars (Hoffman, pg.10).

Another of these resources is time. In reaction to the push for more rigor and high-stakes testing, many states have increased the number of academic courses that students take. Remedial academic education is also on the rise. The number of students planning to attend college continues to grow nationally, which has increased both the numbers and types of academic courses that students are taking. In contrast, the number of CTE courses as compared to the number of academic courses has declined in recent years.

Academic Application

It is sadly ironic that the nationwide movement toward high-stakes academic testing has decreased the perceived value of CTE by many academic-focused educators. The classrooms, laboratories, and student organizations of CTE provide applications for academic concepts. For CTE students, this academic application gives purpose to the need to know these academic concepts. CTE also provides a deeper understanding of related academic concepts, through the illustration of these concepts.

Advocates of the Constructivist theory of learning believe that application is also essential to understanding. Learning that only stresses performance can encourage students to be successful in their academic classes by simply memorizing academic techniques and rules. Without the addition of application, the lack of context, authenticity, and wholeness often leads to poor performance on standardized tests when students are required to recall and demonstrate application proficiency (Brooks and Brooks, pg. 8-9).

One of the goals of high-stakes academic testing is to bring greater levels of student academic success, as evidenced by the goal of increasing the percentages of students required to pass these high-stakes tests. In order to accomplish this goal, schools will need to motivate some students who were not previously motivated. Schools will also need to accommodate a wider range of student learning styles. Career and technical education courses can assist in delivering the understanding of academic subjects to a broader range of student interests and abilities. These courses can provide more concrete explanations of often abstract academic concepts. Students can have the opportunity to see how the concept actually works rather than attempt to imagine it.

This can reinforce academic understanding by repetition and review of the academic concepts as well as by teaching in context. Integration of academic and CTE subject matter in CTE programs was mandated in federal legislation starting in 1990 with Perkins II and continuing through Perkins IV in 2006. The increased levels of contextual understanding offered through applied learning provide a viable venue for increasing rigor for all students. The potential positive effect of integration can be doubled by systematic two-directional integration, where related academic subject matter is applied and integrated into CTE courses while appropriate CTE applications are also integrated into academic courses.

The Successful Practices Network states that one of the ten key components of school improvement is to provide students with real-world applications for academic skills and knowledge (Successful Practices Network, pg. 1). The National Association of Secondary School Principals recommends the utilization of thematic units for creating smaller learning communities as one of their strategies for leading high school reform (NASSP, pg. 8). CTE can be a huge part of this mix. If CTE educators can inform them, academic educators and high school guidance counselors should begin to realize that CTE isn't just for filling in a schedule, not anymore.

Reaching All Students

CTE curriculums and programs have always been designed to successfully reach out to students with diverse abilities and learning styles. Beginning CTE teachers are usually more mature than their academic counterparts and are more likely to have applied experience in their field plus close advisory contact with the workplace of their technical area (Scott and Sarkees-Wircenski, pg. 85). Their contact with persons of diverse academic abilities in the workplace serves to broaden their educational perspective.

In contrast, most incoming high school academic teachers formerly studied alongside high school students with similar abilities and learning styles in college preparation courses, then attended college with students of similar abilities and learning styles, then landed back in high school shortly after graduating from college, and now stand ready to teach what they know. It should come as no surprise that much of their firsthand experience revolves elliptically around college preparation and college requirements.

While a beginning level math teacher may wish for the day when he or she can move up from teaching students enrolled in lower level mathematics to teaching students enrolled in advanced college preparation courses, CTE has long committed their best and most experienced teachers to working with all types of students. It is not unusual to find special needs students mainstreamed in CTE programs and CTSO activities. It is not unusual for these special needs students to be successful in CTE programs and CTSO activities, along with all other types of students.

CTE curriculums are also more likely to use diversified instruction. CTE programs use different instructional venues; this allows them to cater to learning styles that are more varied than just formal teaching. Reardon and Derner suggested that, in general formal teaching settings, the learning that is offered is unlike learning in real life (Reardon and Derner, pg. 9). CTE classrooms and laboratories, however, are designed to duplicate the real-life workplace as closely as possible.

Howard Gardner proposed that there are seven different, or multiple intelligences. J.P. Guilford of the University of Southern California concluded that intelligence is made up of 120 different types of ability (Kagan and Segal, pg. 262). CTE programs have always utilized differentiated learning strategies to address a wide variety of learning intelligences and their companion learning styles. It is not unusual to find certain students who were not doing well in formal settings start to shine as they find different ways to use their other abilities. The results that CTE teachers receive show that they are able to get these students to learn and to promote continued student success. These students form the backbone of technical career areas in the workplace. Their CTE training can help them to become financially successful. Many of them excel in CTSO competitions, and some of them return to become CTE teachers.

Business and Industry Connections

As businesses review their general education needs, they are increasingly demanding more than just academic preparation. Employability skills are being discovered to be important as well. When a 2005 survey for The Manufacturing Institute asked employers if public K-12 schools were doing a good job preparing students for the workplace, 84% responded: *no*. This same survey then asked what were the specific deficiencies in public schools? As expected, 38% of respondents cited Reading and

Comprehension, while 51% cited Math and Science. The highest deficiency cited, however, was Basic Employability Skills at 55% (Deloitte, pg. 16-17). Even at the exploratory or limited credit level, well designed CTE curriculums can comfortably blend these demands into their career training focus.

CTE can also garner the support of business and industry by supporting other types of education - beyond pure academics and support of academics. Upcoming chapters of this book will discuss the importance of the support of business and industry for Career and Technical Student Organizations (CTSOs). This support is also invaluable to CTE. There are many major areas of study in CTE, including Agriscience, Business-Finance-Marketing, Family & Consumer Science, Skilled and Technical Sciences, and Technology Education. In the late twentieth century, CTE experienced an enrollment decline in every CTE major area of study. One area of study (that provides a very specific career focus and facilitates a very close relationship with business and industry) experienced the lowest decline: *Skilled and Technical Sciences* (Gray, pg. 161).

Motivation and Retention

CTE can help to motivate students. Successes gained by students in CTE classes will stimulate more success in high school. Motivated students are easier and more fun to teach. Because motivated students are also more engaged, they are able to learn more. CTE can motivate by demonstrating that an academic concept is relevant by illustrating its practical application. CTE can answer the "Why do we need to know this?" question.

CTE can also explain to some unmotivated students why staying in school is important to their future. Achieve, Inc. is a nonprofit organization devoted to improving rigor and achievement in American high schools. Achieve helped over half of U.S. states benchmark their academic standards and high-stakes testing/accountability systems. Their American Diploma Project proposed that member states make curriculum, standards, and assessment more relevant and engaging by doing more to align them with real-world demands, including post-secondary education and work (The American Diploma Project Network, pg. 8).

One of the concerns of the education community is that pressures of increased high-stakes academic testing will increase the number of students who drop out of high school. Many of these tests are used to determine and limit both promotion and graduation. The fear is that students who are faced with the penalties of being held back from progressing to the next grade and/or graduating may opt out of the system. The percentage of students who fail to complete high school is already significant; data collected by the National Center for Education Statistics (NCES) indicated that the average freshman graduation rate was only 72.6% for the 2001-02 school year (Seastrom, et. al., pg. 2). While referring to the dropout problem as a "silent epidemic", the Alliance for Excellent Education stated that 47% of high school dropouts cited this reason for leaving high school: *Classes were not interesting.* (Bridgeland, et. al., pg. 5).

Taking CTE courses reduces the probability that students will drop out of high school (NAVE Independent Advisory Panel, pg. 13). The National Dropout Prevention Center recommends CTE as one of its stand-alone strategies for dropout prevention (National Dropout Prevention Center/Network, pg. 3). Analyses that were run on the data from the National Educational Longitudinal Study of 1988 showed that the more CTE courses that students took in high school, the lower the probability that they would drop out (Smink and Schargel, pg. 236).

Dale R. Derrickson, Ed.D.

Natural Learning

Human beings are believed to be the result of thousands of years of evolution. A 2003 fossil discovery led the National Science Foundation to report that modern humans may have existed for over 150,000 years (NSF Press Release, pg. 1). Although society has modernized at a continually accelerating rate during the last few hundred years, in the context of evolution, this is a relatively short time period. Our natural way of surviving is still a product of this slow evolution process. How did early man learn? There were no schools. Early man learned by doing, using hands-on learning. This type of learning was not for just a select few who were preparing to move on to formal higher education. Thousands of years ago, every person had no other option than to learn this way. Our human ancestors, who evolved and avoided elimination by natural selection, must have successfully learned this way.

Career and technical education courses offer the opportunity to utilize a more hands-on approach to learning. This can increase student involvement in their education and strengthen student understanding. CTE also broadens the types of student learning styles that can be addressed. It presents many opportunities for differentiated instruction. CTE can foster success for students with other "intelligences" using the strategy of playing to their interests and strengths (Heacox, pg. 23). CTE can offer a level playing field for these students (Hull, pg. 21).

Begin with the End in Mind

Steven Covey urged business management to begin all endeavors with the desired end or destination in mind (Covey, pg. 98). Grant Wiggins and Jay McTighe carried this idea forward for the inheritors of high-stakes testing by proposing that the field of education should utilize this concept (that they expanded and repackaged specifically for educators as "backward design"). They proposed using results-oriented backward design, where designers look at where they want to be before determining how to get there (Wiggins and McTighe, pg. 17). This is something that career and technical educators have done for years; they examined the skills needed for workplace success and sequenced these skills into their planned curriculum.

Educators need to understand that students' futures are currently intertwined with their high-stakes test scores and that CTE can help with this situation, but test scores alone are not the underlying reason for high stakes academic testing. The political and business push behind high-stakes testing was originally aimed at preparing students to compete in the global workplace. Although CTE can assist with preparing students for academic testing, CTE educators additionally have a century of experience developing curriculum based on the needs of the workplace. This experience can be easily conveyed to students to help motivate them to begin educational endeavors by illustrating the opportunities for workplace success.

Workplace success is the end that should be in the mind of high school students. Whether students intend to enter the workplace full-time immediately after graduation, whether students intend to enter post-secondary education immediately, or whether students intend to enter both the workplace and post-secondary education immediately after completing high school, they need career guidance to help them select a high skill, high wage career pathway that is in high demand. Students need to be aware of educational labor market opportunities in order to be able to make informed career and educational choices (ACTE Position Paper, pg. 10). CTE plays a huge role in this process. High school career programs can provide career training for job-entry and help students to select or continue a viable post-secondary education major for a future job.

Quality

If critics complain that a particular CTE program is not providing many of the benefits outlined in the overview, this does not mean that CTE is not a beneficial form of education. It only means that the particular program needs to improve its quality, for it is not delivering the full array of benefits to its students. This does not mean that adding a CTSO element to any particular program will automatically improve the quality of the program. CTSOs are not the sole determinant of quality; however, CTE programs that do not utilize CTSOs as part of their education strategy are lacking a vital quality component.

If teachers of CTE programs feel that they already provide all of the previously listed benefits for their students without the inclusion of the CTSO component, the addition of CTSO activities to all that is already being done might be questioned. It is also possible that teachers who comfortably include some, but not all, of the CTSO component will question the benefit of doing more. The following two ideas will be reinforced in upcoming chapters:

1. Programs offering all of the previous CTE benefits (without offering all possible CTSO benefits) must have hard-working teachers. Although initiating or increasing CTSO activities as a required integral part of their curriculum will mean additional work at first, this extra effort will fade after the teachers implement activities. The net result of this effort will slowly become zero additional work for a time, but as teachers learn to get the students more involved, the work load can shift. The students can begin to assume a leadership role in these activities which can enable them to take over more of the operation and management of these activities. When that happens, the net result of implementing CTSO activities will then begin to lessen the teacher-advisors' workload.

2. Programs offering CTE benefits with incomplete or no participation in CTSO activities must have dedicated teachers. If their teachers initiate or increase CTSO activities, they will find that they are able to greatly expand and enhance the CTE benefits that they already offer to their students. When these teachers reach the point that their students are helping to lead these activities, these teacher-advisors will find that they have more time to concentrate on the art and science of quality teaching.

Chapter Two

History of National Organizations

"History is philosophy teaching from examples."
Dionysius of Halicarnassus

Early American Progress

To understand the history of national career and technical student organizations (CTSOs) for secondary education requires a rudimentary understanding of the history of secondary career and technical education (CTE). When public education started to evolve in the United States, its purpose was to promote civics and academics. Manual training (an earlier name for CTE) was not a part of early secondary education.

Apprenticeships were a precursor to public CTE. In apprenticeship's initial American form, the apprentice often left his family to live with and under the strict control of the master craftsman for several years. The arrival of the Industrial revolution in the 19th century actually caused a decline in apprenticeship (Finch and Crunkilton, pg. 5). As the nation grew and industrial revolution progressed, opportunities for non-skilled employment created a competition for entry-level employees who often viewed factory employment as a more free and less controlled alternative to the apprenticed positions that were available. The need for employees with technical training would eventually overcome the ability of the apprenticeship system to continue to provide enough workers with the appropriate technical skills.

The 1876 Centennial Exposition was held in Fairmount Park, Philadelphia. The latest technology of the Industrial Revolution was on display. Some of these displays became part of the Smithsonian Institution collection in our nation's capital. Victor Della Vos, director of the Imperial Technical School of Moscow, was also there to demonstrate the latest approach to teaching the mechanical arts (Finch and Crunkilton, pg. 5). This may have been the first time that so many American educators had seen such an organized approach to curriculum for career-based technical arts.

Morrill Acts of 1862 and 1890

The first federal legislation that promoted occupational education was a public college initiative (Wenrich et. al., pg. 24). U.S. Representative Justin Morrill of Vermont introduced legislation to create a system of state universities that would prepare teachers and train students for agriculture and the mechanical arts (Scott and Sarkees-Wircenski, pg. 142). The Morrill Act of 1862 directed the federal government to donate 30,000 acres of public lands to each state. The states could sell these lands to endow and operate at least one college. The purpose of the colleges "shall be, without excluding other scientific and classical studies and including military tactics, to teach such branches of learning as are related to agriculture and the mechanical arts, in order to promote the liberal and practical education of the industrial classes in several pursuits and professions in life" (NASULGC, pg. 17). The Morrill Act of 1890 provided $15,000 to each state to support these land-grant colleges (Finch and McGough, pg. 24).

In spite of these developments, William T. Harris, who was U.S. Commissioner of Education from 1889 to 1906, expressed the view that manual training could be supported in public secondary schools, but it must be regulated to stand in last place behind citizenship and purely academic subjects (Barlow, pg. 17).

Smith Acts

U.S. Senator Hoke Smith of Georgia co-sponsored several pieces of legislation related to CTE promoting agriculture extension, home economics, World War I veterans' training, and the training of disabled persons (Scott and Sarkees-Wircenski, pg. 434-435). His co-sponsored 1917 legislation is the best known and most significant.

In 1914, a joint resolution of Congress resulted in Senator Smith being named as chairman of a commission to study federal aid to vocational education. The recommendations of this commission were incorporated into federal legislation. U.S. Representative Dudley Hughes of Georgia added a revision to include home economics as an eligible fund recipient (Scott and Sarkees-Wircenski, pg. 171-172). Their Smith-Hughes legislation passed in 1917.

The Smith-Hughes National Vocational Education Act of 1917 marked the beginning of a nationwide push for increasing the availability and quality of public occupationally-based secondary education (Finch and McGough, pg. 25). This initiative continues through current Perkins legislation. The Smith-Hughes Act did not mention creation or support for student organizations. CTSOs, as we know them, did not exist at the time. In spite of these facts, Smith-Hughes did have a tremendous effect on the creation of what were first categorized as Vocational Student Organizations (VSOs).

After courses in vocational education were encouraged nationwide by Smith-Hughes, the first idea of an organization for vocational students seemed to naturally evolve at the grassroots level in agriculture, trades and industry, and home economics education. This need was filled by local chapters before the first national organizations were formed. As other forms of CTE became part of public education, the evolution of their organizations built upon the success of earlier student organizations.

FFA

Although increased industrialization and urbanization of America had reduced the percentage of farmers at the end of the 19th century, farming remained a strong economic and political force. As late as 1930, twenty-five percent of the population still lived on farms (Boyle, pg. 3). The passage of the Hatch Act in 1887 had created agricultural experimental stations through the nation's land-grant colleges. The 1914 Smith-Lever Act supported cooperative extension efforts in agriculture that systematized the movement of this agricultural knowledge from colleges to the farms (NASULGC, pg. 16). It was the Smith-Hughes Act of 1917 that brought agricultural education into the realm of the public secondary school (Giachino & Gallington, pg. 15).

FFA was started in secondary schools at the grassroots level. The first known clubs were formed in the State of Virginia in the early 1920s. The Virginia Future Farmers club was an innovation that spread across the country quickly without the umbrella of a national organization. After more states became involved, the national organization was born in 1928 at the Baltimore Hotel in Kansas City, Missouri as the Future Farmers of America. In 1950, FFA was officially chartered by the U.S. Government in PL740, the Act to Incorporate the Future Farmers of America (Scott and Sarkees-Wircenski, pg. 291). Although the official name of the national organization was slightly changed to the National FFA Organization in 1988, FFA is the oldest national organization that has remained in continuous operation (FFA, pg. 5).

Agricultural education has moved beyond simply farming. Today, it is more commonly known as agriscience. Agriscience represents a broad range of agricultural and food science occupations. FFA chapters continue to operate for Agriscience students, and they are in place at many educational levels. Students of these chapters can be found wearing the distinctive blue FFA corduroy jacket in middle schools, high schools, colleges, and universities.

FCCLA

The Chicago World's Fair of 1893 had stimulated an interest in domestic sciences and home economics. An investigation studying the scope of this field and the development of educational subject matter led to the founding of the American Home Economics Association in 1899 (Walter, pg.8-9). The 1914 Smith-Lever Act also supported cooperative extension efforts in home economics (NASULGC, pg. 16). By the early 1920s, a variety of local school clubs had begun. Some of these clubs were part of a state organization. The only national affiliation that any of these clubs had was that some of them were sponsored by the American Home Economics Association (FCCLA, pg. 19).

In 1945, the Bankhead-Flannagan Act provided for further development of home economics cooperative extension (NASULGC, pg. 17). FCCLA began as the Future Homemakers of America (FHA) in the same year that the Bankhead-Flannagan Act passed. This organization was founded to serve the needs of Home Economics teachers and students in states where schools were not segregated. A parallel organization, the New Homemakers of America, was founded to serve black students in the 16 states where schools were segregated by state law (FCCLA, pg. 20). The New Homemakers of America organization merged with FHA in 1965, shortly after the passage of the Civil Rights Act of 1964. In 1971, FHA expanded to include Home Economics Related Occupations (HERO) chapters (FCCLA, pg. 21).

Proponents of home economics had modernized their purposes by the 1990s. Soon after, they began to modernize their image. In 1995, FHA/HERO changed their bylaws so that all references to "home economics" were replaced by "family and consumer sciences" (FCCLA, pg. 25). In light of this, FHA/HERO re-examined the name of their national student organization. FHA restated their new purpose when they updated their name in 1999 to the Family, Career, and Community Leaders of America or FCCLA (FCCLA, pg. 26). FCCLA currently calls their competitions STAR Events, representing Students Taking Action with Recognition (STAR).

SkillsUSA

Trade and Industrial teachers and students formed the Future Craftsmen of America in the 1920's. Unfortunately, this early organization only provided two years of national conventions before it ended. Trade and industrial education did not disappear; by 1934, the George-Ellzey Act added Trade and Industrial education to the list of CTE areas supported by federal funding (Walter, pg. 12).

The operation of clubs at the local level continued, and in 1960 state supervisors of trade and industrial education reported 799 local trade and industrial clubs in eighteen states. With the backing of the U.S. Office of Education and the American Vocational Association (AVA-now the Association for Career and Technical Education or ACTE), the Vocational Industrial Clubs of America (VICA) national organization was formed in 1965 (SkillsUSA, pg. 22 and 23). As the national contests for this organization grew, the contests at their national conference became known as the United States Skills Olympics.

In 1995, national competitions were held under the new name "SkillsUSA Championships" (SkillsUSA, pg. 26). On July 4, 1999 VICA incorporated this change and updated the name of the organization to SkillsUSA-VICA. This intermediate change helped the public to continue to follow the organization by name. In the final analysis, it was part of an overall plan to completely update the name. On September 1, 2004 this change was completed when the organization's name became simply SkillsUSA.

In 2005, the National Association of State Supervisors of Trade and Industrial Education (NASSTIE) decided to merge with the National Association for Trade and Industry Education (NATIE). As a result of this merger, a new name was created for Trade and Industrial Education that more adequately represented the new technologies in this branch of CTE: Skilled and Technical Sciences (STS). The name of the new organization that formed as a result of the merger became the Association for Skilled and Technical Sciences (ASTS).

FBLA

The initial form of the Future Business Leaders of America (FBLA) was developed in 1937 by Dr. Hamden L. Forkner at the Teachers College of Columbia University and sponsored in 1940 by the National Council for Business Education. The first high school chapter of FBLA was chartered in 1942. The first chapter of FBLA's post-secondary division, Phi Beta Lambda (PBL), was chartered in 1958 (FBLA-PBL, pg. 5).

Business education was a viable CTE choice for public high school students, and FBLA was started due to a perceived need for a national student organization to serve locally-organized business clubs in high schools. FBLA-PBL has expanded their service so that it currently benefits students in middle school, high school, and post-secondary education (Camp et.al., pg. 14-15).

DECA

DECA was founded to serve marketing education or distributive education students. Many education programs in the late 1930s and early 1940s used part-time employment out of the school setting at business training sites for distributive education. To counter the lack of central organization for these CTE programs, local marketing/retailing education clubs were often formed. Some states even sponsored statewide conferences for these students. The United States Office of Education and AVA (now ACTE) worked with state supervisors of distributive education to create a national organization beginning in 1946 (DECA, pg. I-4).

The first national conference, the Interstate Conference of Distributive Education Clubs, was held in 1947. The DECA name, Distributive Education Clubs of America, was adopted at the second national conference in 1948. By 1953 DECA had established their first national headquarters (DECA, pg. I-5). Over the years, this organization worked to assist and improve marketing, management, and entrepreneurship education. To reflect their original mission and minimize confusion over their name, this organization has modified their name to "DECA, An Association of Marketing Students".

DECA also has a post-secondary division. In 1961, this Junior College Division was established for post-secondary marketing education students enrolled in college programs that provided degrees other than bachelors or graduate degrees. The name of this division was updated to Delta Epsilon Chi in 1982. The program is now open to students pursuing a bachelors degree (DECA, pg. I-7).

BPA

The Vocational Act of 1963 eliminated the direction of federal funding toward specific career areas. States were instead given the freedom to direct funds toward CTE as needed by the changing demands of the labor market. This facilitated the growth of diversity in CTE (Walter, pg. 15). Office education grew in the states, and American Vocational Association surveys of state supervisors of office education confirmed the desire for an organization serving the needs of office occupations students. As a result, the Vocational Office Education Clubs of America (VOECA) was created in 1966 (Camp et.al., pg. 11). This quickly evolved into the Office Education Association (OEA). The evolution of names continued into 1988, when the Office Education Association updated their name to the Business Professionals of America (Delaware BPA, pg. 4).

The similarities of the types of students served by FBLA, DECA, and BPA might be seen by some to be conducive to a merger of these organizations, but that has not yet happened and may or may not occur in the future. Each of these entities stands alone as a complete and dynamic organization.

TSA

In 1958, the American Industrial Arts Association (AIAA) sponsored the American Industrial Arts Student Association (AIASA) for industrial arts students. AIASA operated as a part of AIAA for twenty years. AIASA, Inc. was formed as a stand-alone vocational student organization in 1978. The organization operated successfully for many years as AIAA, but the equipment and skills needed by industry changed drastically over time. Industrial arts education curriculum modernized to absorb many new technologies. As a result, industrial arts education evolved to become technology education. In 1988, AIASA updated their name to reflect this ongoing evolution. The new organization is now called the Technology Student Association or TSA (TSA, pg. 1).

HOSA

The healthcare field is a growing occupational area. Many of the diverse healthcare occupations have shortages of skilled workers. Healthcare training is an important part of today's CTE. Healthcare CTE students are served by two organizations: SkillsUSA and the Health Occupations Students of America (HOSA). The SkillsUSA organization, which started as VICA in 1965, serves the needs of some healthcare students through their Health Occupations Contests. These contests cover general healthcare skills as well as dental assisting, medical assisting, and nursing. SkillsUSA also includes non-healthcare trade, industrial, and technical contests. The history of SkillsUSA has been explored previously. HOSA focuses exclusively on healthcare. It also has its own unique history.

Future Nurses Clubs also served some of the early demand for a vocational student organization at the local level. As interest grew, several states started state organizations that served health occupations students exclusively. In 1975, these states formed the American Health Occupations Education Student Organization. In 1976, they held their Constitutional Convention where they shortened the official name to Health Occupations Students of America (HOSA Handbook: Section A, pg. 33-35).

George Acts

U.S. Senator Walter F. George from Georgia co-sponsored four pieces of federal legislation that supported early CTE and CTSOs over three decades and were known as the "George Acts" (Camp, et.al., pg. 7). The George-Reed Act of 1929 provided appropriations for home economics and agriculture through 1934. The George-Ellzey Act of 1934 extended the 1929 appropriations at an increased level and added trade and industrial education to federally-funded vocational education. The George-Deen Act of 1936 increased funding and added distributive education to federally-funded vocational programs (Walter, pg. 13).

The first three "George Acts" added to the types of vocational education programs that would be entitled to receive federal funding. These acts also increased the amount of funding for these programs. The final act, the George-Barden Act of 1946, also increased funding, but it added a new twist. The George-Barden Act was the first federal legislation to specifically designate funds for a vocational student organization for agricultural students (Camp, et.al., pg. 7).

Perkins Acts

The Vocational Education Act of 1963 (AKA Perkins-Morse Bill) increased funding for secondary and post-secondary vocational education programs as it altered the mandate of federal education support to meet the demands of accelerating change in the labor market. U.S. Representative Carl D. Perkins from Kentucky played an influential role in the passage of this law (ACTE, pg. 11). As the act moved toward reauthorization, he maintained his influence on CTE legislation as Chairman of the Committee on Education and Labor. The result of the reauthorization was a new act that was named the Carl D. Perkins Act of 1984 (also known as Perkins I). Perkins I introduced the objective to improve access to programs and the quality of programs for special populations, as well as improving the quality and economic impact of all vocational education programs (Walter, pg. 17).

Although Representative Perkins died in 1984, his legacy lives on through further extensions of his CTE advocacy. The next revision was named the Carl D. Perkins Vocational and Applied Technology Act of 1990 (Perkins II). Perkins II introduced the requirement that curricula integrate vocational and academic methodologies (AVA, pg. 78). The third version, the Carl D. Perkins Vocational and Technical Act of 1998 (Perkins III), launched the state performance accountability system for vocational and technical education (Brustein and Mahler, pg. 30). The fourth version, the Carl D. Perkins Career and Technical Education Act of 2006 (Perkins IV), continued the accountability system while adding local accountability.

Filling a Need

While each of the career and technical student organizations has a slightly different origin, they each grew out of a need to serve students in CTE programs. The fact that some of these national organizations began as school-level clubs is very important. Early CTE teachers recognized the potential of this type of co-curricular activity to broaden and increase both the motivation and the education of their students. These pioneers had to create their own structure and materials. In these beginnings, the opportunities and prestige of their organizations did not extend to the national level. Nevertheless, these ground-breaking teachers incorporated their localized versions of CTE into their CTSO activities.

This natural relationship of CTE and CTSOs meant that these pioneers must have used the CTSO activities to enhance what they were already doing in their classrooms and laboratories. When their CTSO activities were initiated, they must have been designed to reflect what was taught. These activities were pulled from curriculum. To do that, they must have been embedded in the curriculum.

New career and technical education teachers, especially those who have had little or no previous exposure to CTSOs, may initially view co-curricular CTSO activities as just one more thing being required of an already busy day. These activities were created by someone else, so they may see the general relationships to their curricular objectives without seeing the opportunities to embed all or part of an activity into what they teach. It is the function of this text to explain the purpose and possibility of these organizations for teachers as well as students. Once an understanding of the function of these organizations is fully gained, a realization generally follows for good teachers: if CTSOs didn't already exist, we would need to invent them.

Chapter Three

Goals of National Organizations

"When schemes are laid in advance, it is surprising
how often the circumstances fit in with them."
Sir William Osler

Planned Outcomes

While they are specific to the occupational outcomes of the type of CTE that they support, the general objectives of all CTSOs have some similarities. When statements or sections of statements that apply only to a specific group of careers are deleted, many of the remaining statements could be applied to other organizations. The following statements leave out some of the occupational-specific CTSOs' objectives to illustrate this point.

BPA has a mission statement that reads:

> *The mission of Business Professionals of America is to contribute to the preparation of a world-class workforce through the advancement of leadership, citizenship, academic, and technological skills.* (BPA, pg. 5)

DECA's mission statement contains the both specific and non-specific ideas: *to enhance the co-curricular education of students…develop career skills and competence, build self-esteem, experience leadership, and practice community service* (DECA, pg. 1-3).

FBLA also has goals that relate to providing opportunities for students to:

- ☐ *Strengthen the confidence of students in themselves and their work*

- ☐ *Develop character, prepare for useful citizenship, and foster patriotism*

- ☐ *Encourage scholarship and promote school loyalty*

- ☐ *Facilitate the transition from school to work* (FBLA, pg. 1)

FCCLA's mission mentions the promotion of personal growth and leadership development for its members. FCCLA also lists purposes of its organization that could be used for organizations that do not also promote family and consumer science:

> *1. To provide opportunities for personal development and preparation for adult life;…*

Dale R. Derrickson, Ed.D.

2. *To encourage democracy through cooperative action in the home and community;*

3. *To encourage individual and group involvement in helping achieve global cooperation and harmony;*

4. *To promote greater understanding between youth and adults;*

5. *To provide opportunities for making decisions and for assuming responsibilities;*

6. *To prepare for the multiple roles of men and women in today's society;...* (FCCLA, pg. ii)

FFA outlines the objectives of their organization in their constitution and bylaws. Highlighting non-specific objectives reveals that they propose:

1. *To be an integral part of the organized instructional programs...*

2. *To strengthen the confidence of students in themselves and in their work by developing desirable work habits and effective usage of their time; by learning to assume responsibility; and by developing competencies in communications, human relations, and other social abilities leading to the intelligent choice of a career...*

3. *To provide...programs and activities which will develop pride, responsibility, leadership, character, scholarship, citizenship, patriotism, and thrift...*

4. *To encourage and recognize achievement...* (FFA, pg. 67)

HOSA lists the goals for each member of their organization. The generic goals are as follows:

- *To promote physical, mental, and social well being.*

- *To develop effective leadership qualities and skills.*

- *To develop the ability to communicate more effectively with people.*

- *To develop character.*

- *To develop responsible citizenship traits.*

- *To understand the importance of pleasing oneself as well as being of service to others.*

- *To build self-confidence and pride in one's work.*

- *To develop an understanding of the importance of interacting and cooperating with other students and organizations.*

- *To encourage individual and group achievement.* (HOSA, pg. 7)

SkillsUSA provides a list of purposes for their organization. When the purposes that are specific to trade and industrial education and health occupations education are deleted, these purposes remain:

- *To develop leadership abilities through participation in educational, vocational, civic, recreational and social activities*

- *To foster a deep respect for the dignity of work*

- *To assist students in establishing realistic vocational goals*

- *To help students attain a purposeful life*

- *To create enthusiasm for learning*

- *To promote high standards in trade ethics, workmanship, scholarship, and safety*

- *To develop the ability of students to plan together, organize and carry out worthy activities and projects through the use of the democratic process*

- *To foster a wholesome understanding of the functions of labor and management organizations and a recognition of their mutual interdependence*

- *To develop patriotism through knowledge of our nation's heritage and the practice of democracy* (SkillsUSA, pg. 4)

TSA communicates their mission in a short, but effectively complete statement:

The mission of the Technology Student Association is to prepare for the challenges of a dynamic world by promoting technological literacy, leadership, and problem solving, resulting in personal growth and opportunities. (TSA, pg. v.)

Direct Leadership

How important to a student's future is leadership participation? Leadership encompasses not only organizational and management skills, but it also can include developing self-control and accentuating personal direction. For some students, it can mean the opportunity to build enough self-confidence by learning and practicing interaction skills that will enable these students to step out of the shadows, to correctly speak up, and to begin to get involved. For other students, it may provide the opportunity to hone existing skills.

Every CTSO mentions leadership when describing the planned outcomes of their organization. They propose to promote and stimulate interest in leadership, to provide opportunities for students to experience leadership activities, and/or to develop and advance leadership skills. The exact wording for each of these descriptions is not as important as the inclusion of the word "leadership" in their plans.

CTSOs do provide <u>direct</u> opportunities for students to become leaders. From national officer teams, to state officer teams, to local chapter officer teams - there are many leadership positions that are created by these organizations for their students. There are many categories of these positions that can provide direct leadership experience:

1. President

2. Vice President(s)

3. Secretary

4. Treasurer

5. Parliamentarian

6. Historian

7. Reporter

Not every CTSO has every one of these positions in their officer teams, but all CTSOs use many of these. In addition to becoming an officer, other opportunities to act as a leader may arise. CTSOs may form committees and/or sub-committees to carry out their work plans.

Becoming elected or appointed to a leadership position in a CTSO at any level gives the student an opportunity to experience leadership and strengthen their leadership abilities through their direct exposure to these leadership positions. When students are elected to a leadership position, their advisors usually offer training at the inception of their term of office. This training helps to make these direct leadership activities even more meaningful. While training may be a day or week in length at the beginning of their term, ongoing coaching of these student leaders continues to assist in the polishing of their leadership skills.

Indirect Leadership

What sort of attributes should be learned and practiced by a good leader? Public speaking, written communication, parliamentary procedure, teamwork, project planning, and project management are just a few of the skills that might serve future leaders well. These same skills will also assist future employees who may not start their careers in a leadership position. CTSO students do not have to be elected to be exposed to opportunities to gain and polish these skills. These skills can be learned and practiced indirectly by student participation in activities that are based on leadership attributes.

CTSOs have designed opportunities for all of their students to develop and practice their leadership skills. These opportunities are found in the competitions of the CTSOs. Sometimes referred to as leadership competitions, these activities are available to help increase student leadership participation.

Each contest focuses indirectly on at least one leadership skill area. Some of the emphasized skills are:

1. Public Presentations

2. Written Documentation

3. Ceremonial Rituals

4. Public Service Endeavors

5. Knowledge Bowls

6. Display Projects

7. Skill Demonstrations

8. Parliamentary Procedures

9. Team Activities

Students participating in these activities may or may not also be elected officers of their CTSO at the local, regional, state, or national level. Either way, these students are able to learn and expand their leadership skills indirectly, without being elected to an office.

Respect and Rewards

Grant Wiggins and Jay McTighe advocate using a results-oriented backward design approach to educational design, where designers look at where they want to be before determining how to get there (Wiggins and McTighe, pg. 17). This is something that many career and technical educators have done for years; they examined the skills needed to be successful in the workplace and sequenced these skills into their planned curriculum. It is no mistake that CTSOs incorporate awards and recognition into their plans. This did not occur as an afterthought to contests and other activities that involve recognition.

In their objectives, CTSOs propose to create enthusiasm and encourage achievement. The availability of recognition and awards provides a level of motivation for students to give their best effort when participating in activities that lead directly to an award. The celebration of the awarding of certificates and/or other prizes recognizes the achievements of students to continue this motivation. Thousands of dollars' worth of medals, prizes, and scholarships are often awarded to winning students at state and national conferences. The distribution of less expensive awards at local competitions can still provide great motivation. The positive effect of this recognition can greatly exceed the expense of the items given.

CTSOs propose to foster respect for their occupational area as well as to provide recognition for their membership. One of the ways that they foster respect is also through the recognition of students. The honoring of student occupational skills in recognition ceremonies enhances the respect for the career area. When business and industry personnel are able to be a part of the process of judging or recognizing students, this process brings a new perspective to the worth of the skills that students are practicing.

The CTSOs themselves elevate the level of pride for an occupational area just by the purpose for their existence. CTSOs are the moral equivalent of national professional and trade organizations for students in their respective career areas. They can enhance the levels of professional esteem for their members in their community in the same way that business and industry professional and trade organizations work to increase pride and respect inside their organizations and in the public eye.

Citizenship and Community

CTSOs are patriotic organizations. Many of their official ceremonies incorporate patriotic statements and symbolism. U.S. and state flags are usually displayed during ceremonies. The Pledge of Allegiance may be recited and/or the Star Spangled Banner may be played or even sung. The words "citizenship", "democracy", and "patriotism" are found in many ceremonies and goals. When chapters meet and plan their program of work, these meetings reflect the same aura of democracy in action that is found in student government meetings.

The promotion of citizenship is an integral part of CTSO operations, and students are consistently exposed to this incorporation. When some students participate, they may feel highly patriotic as a result. Other students may not be as moved by these patriotic displays, but the patriotic perspective of CTSOs will be a positive influence on students. This is not the only way that these organizations can help students to learn how to become responsible citizens in their community.

CTSO meetings use standard parliamentary procedure to carry out their meetings. This could occur at a national officer meeting or a local chapter meeting. All CTSO members should have the opportunity to attend meetings for their organization. Exposure to these meetings can help students begin to learn how to participate in meetings using the standards of meeting conduct in a less intimidating setting than many civic meetings. This introduction can make them more able to participate in community activities and government when they become adults.

CTSOs also value public service. Some competitions are based on developing, carrying-out, and documenting a public service project. In addition to this contest avenue, CTSO students often participate in public service activities at the local, state, and/or national level. These non-competitive activities are often encouraged and guided by CTSO advisors, although the students may decide to get involved or to increase their chapter's involvement as part of their CTSO plan of work.

Technical Skill Enhancement

Examining the common threads of these separate, but similar organizations provides stark clues as to why these organizations can be an important part of career and technical curriculum for the area that they represent. Preparing, developing, and promoting growth for students certainly fits the instructional goals of any type of education. Motivating students is certainly important in the education of students. But is there more?

For the CTE aspect of a high school student's education, the technical skill activities found in CTSO contests offer an opportunity for students to practice and display their technical skills. One important advantage is often overlooked. As students advance through a training program, they learn many technical competencies that they can bring to the workplace. Depending on the duration of the CTE program, these skill sets may be few or many. When the length of the program involves multiple years, students may tend not to be as current in a particular skill or set of skills as the workplace may demand.

Asking students to "do over" a skill demonstration that they learned in a previous year or years may not be an inspiring idea to them. CTSO contests offer teachers another way to review and practice skill competencies. Because the perspective is changed from review to competition, this can provide more motivation for students to review their skills as part of the CTSO contest participation. Teachers can incorporate these activities to provide for a well-disguised review.

Technical skills are not the only skills that can be reviewed in contest activities. Leadership skills can be practiced using the contest format. These contests also integrate many science, mathematics, and English language arts concepts into their make-up. Review of these academic skills often takes place during contest preparation and participation. It is not unusual to find some innovative academic teachers coaching their students in concert with the CTE teachers in preparation for contests. In certain leadership contests, academic teachers are able to join in the judging as well.

Connections with Business and Industry

The first national student organization for trade and industrial students was the Future Craftsmen of America. Had this organization persevered, it possibly would have evolved into some form of the SkillsUSA organization. Yet this organization lasted only two years. The reason for the early demise of this organization was not insufficient purpose or inadequate utility. This organization failed because it did not have the support of the business community (SkillsUSA, pg. 22). All CTSOs can serve as a conduit to assist CTE educators who see the necessity of connecting business and education closer together. Career and technical educators should have an acute awareness of the importance of the business connection to CTE and to CTSOs.

Why would business and industry representatives want to participate in CTSOs? If CTE programs direct students toward high demand careers (as encouraged in Perkins IV), many employers are willing to participate because they need appropriately skilled workers. Some of these employers' representatives already lend their expertise to CTE advisory committees to help keep CTE on-track and up-to-date so that CTE educators are able to train these future workers appropriately.

The participation of these representatives as advisors and judges continues their CTE interaction and input. This participation is invaluable to CTSO contests and activities. When these contests and activities are properly represented as an important, co-curricular aspect of CTE, business and industry advisory representatives are more easily recruited.

Some businesses are also willing to donate financial assets that are needed to operate organizations, provide contests, subsidize student entry fees, and/or supply awards. These donations are always charitable and usually deductible, but they are not out of context with other necessary expenses incurred by a profit-driven business. Businesses can be willing to pay $10,000 a year or more to educate an intern or an apprentice because they understand this to be an investment in human capital (Gordon, pg. 208). CTSOs facilitate skill training, and businesses see the value of that training for potential employees. CTSOs also seek to instill pride in the student for their career area, and that increases the chances that students who are hired will remain in that profession and not waste on-the-job training expenditures.

Motivation

Another benefit to students and teachers is simply the motivation that these organizations can provide for students. It may seem repetitive to mention motivation because it has been part of previously

Dale R. Derrickson, Ed.D.

discussed aspects of the purposes of CTSOs. Perhaps so, but motivation is too important to gloss over. Motivation plays a key role in achievement (Goleman, pg. 79).

Many high school students show little interest in education because they fail to see the connection between what is taught and their world. When adults consider the distractions of working after school and on weekends (plus personal electronic devices, television, talking with friends, and text messaging), teenagers have many activities to occupy their attention. Disinterested students can drop out of high school completely, or they can disengage while continuing to attend. Either choice can be tantamount to poisoning their education experience.

Quality career and technical programs already show real-world applications of their focused skills and general academic skills. This connection fosters increased student understanding which cultivates enthusiasm and persistence. CTEs can positively impact drop-out rates. CTSOs can be an important part of increasing the motivation of CTE students, but it requires effort. Why should a teacher try to do more by adding on career and technical student organization activities?

Co-curricular

First, career and technical student organization activities are not designed to be an add-on. They are engineered to be an integral part of the curriculum. They should not detract from what teachers are trying to accomplish. CTSOs should be a part of what teachers are doing, and they should complement what teachers are trying to accomplish. Once teachers have embedded selected career and technical student organization activities in their curriculums, these become a natural extension of day-to-day activities. Once properly incorporated, they can't be separated without leaving a hole in the curriculum.

Second, top quality career and technical programs already make full use of career and technical student organization activities in their curriculum activities. The effort to raise the quality of these programs led to the original grass-roots foundation of career and technical student organizations. The pioneers must have realized that creating student organizations would upgrade the quality of their instruction. Those that followed surely used the model of the pioneers to forge their organizations, but they also used the successes of the pioneers as a foundation for the ideals and goals of their organizations. But how can CTSO activities add to the successes of career and technical education programs?

Analogy

Perhaps this comparison will assist in explaining. Imagine that basketball was a realistic career opportunity for large numbers of students (with average or slightly above average athletic abilities) in every school district in the country. So basketball would be taught in large numbers of high schools across the country as a career and technical subject that would lead to lifetime employment. Imagine also that there was no interscholastic basketball league (student organization). Then imagine that basketball was initially taught in the following manner to prepare students to gain only individual knowledge and skills.

First students would study the history of basketball. Then they would study the rules of basketball. They would also study and practice individual fundamentals, such as dribbling, shooting, and rebounding their own shot. Occasionally, two students would practice the fundamentals of guarding and shot-blocking against each other, but there would be no practice as a team - especially in preparation for a game. No scrimmages or games, just study and individual or semi-individual practice of the fundamentals. Teachers would fully be able to comprehend the value of teaching the fundamentals, but some students would be slightly bored and not highly motivated.

Now imagine that the basketball teachers got together and formed a student organization, the Interscholastic Basketball Students of America. This organization would promote teamwork skills through playing games at the national, state and local level. It would bring the schools and the community together to watch the games. It would provide recognition and prizes for the students. It would emphasize sportsmanship in addition to technical knowledge and skills. It would bring together national experts to formulate rules and regulations for a national contest which would set a national skill standard for all activities.

Under this student organization, students would practice to play games at the school level. Before each game, they would scrimmage to hone their skills in this local competition. After each game, they would work to improve their skills before the next game. Each team would strive to reach the regional and/or state level of competition; each team that made the state level would attempt to reach the national level. All students would receive certificates of participation, and some students could win local, regional, state, and/or national medals. After graduation, these students would use their experience to gain employment in the thriving basketball industry. Meanwhile, they would experience some of that industry's reality while still in high school.

This scenario improves student interest greatly after the addition of the student organization. It improves and expands both student learning and student motivation. It offers students another opportunity to get in the game. This connectivity is good for the students, and what is good for the students can be very good for the teacher. A motivated student makes the teaching experience much better. The organization also provides a base of nationally-recognized competency standards.

Employers would be involved at every stage. They would help to formulate standards. They would support and judge competitions. They would recognize and hire students who were active in this student organization. The greater their demand for employees out of this system, the stronger would be their motivation to support this endeavor. Eventually, the students coming out of this system would be in industry positions where they could lend support from their perspective as well.

Whatever extra work the teachers did to integrate the activities of this student organization into the curriculum was offset by the efficiency gained by the increase in student motivation. In fact, the greatest burden was creating the organization. For teachers participating in BPA, DECA, FCCLA, FBLA, FFA, HOSA, SkillsUSA, and TSA, that burden has been lifted.

Chapter Four

State and National Curriculum Requirements and Resources

"Whoever has the gold makes all the rules."

Original Source Unknown

Combination of Requirements

Integrating career and technical student organization activities into CTE programs is a requirement, typically at some combination of the Federal, State, and local level. If the word requirement brings to mind the image of students trying to have a positive experience in an activity where the teacher is being forced to participate, remember that where CTSO incorporation into the curriculum is mandated, the primary reason is to improve educational experiences for students. The overwhelming majority of career and technical education teachers want to provide a quality educational experience for their students. Therefore it is expected that when good teachers learn about the benefits of CTSOs, they will want to afford these benefits to their students. When good teachers work to embed the principles, activities, and goals of student organizations into their curriculum, there are requirements that will justify what they are doing with CTSOs to their administration.

U.S. Constitution & Local Control

The United States Constitution provides the framework for government responsibilities and control in this country. The Constitution was written in 1787 and completed in 1791 with the addition of the Bill of Rights (National Constitution Center, pg. 1). The completed Constitution does not specifically mention public education due to the fact that it preceded the launch of widespread public education in the next century. Since the Constitution does not specifically mention public education, it is generally assumed that public education is under the control of the states due to the Tenth Amendment. The Tenth Amendment declares that powers not delegated to the federal government by the Constitution or prohibited by the Constitution would be reserved to the states or to the people. Most of the states have delegated some of their authority to the local control of district school boards. As a result, some people erroneously assume that public education is completely under state and/or local control.

Funding Requirements

U.S. public education is frequently viewed starting as decentralized framework with local school boards directing policy for their district. Policy can include local tax rates, staff contracts, hiring, and student-achievement goals. This local influence and control is considered essential to maintaining schools that reflect community needs and values. School districts must also adhere to state regulations, as they usually derive their authority and/or some portion of their funding from their state. State funding may also come with state mandates and requirements which can include state testing. Although limited in application, a U.S. state or territorial entity may also choose to have a statewide school district.

Of course, school districts must also comply with federal laws when they accept federal funds. For example, local school districts must participate in mandated testing. In some states, this testing may have purely been a state initiative before it became a federal mandate in the No Child Left Behind Act of 2001. After the federal mandate, states were required to implement state testing in a federally-approved format that complies with federal requirements. When there is a federal legislation, districts must comply with that law or risk being in violation of the law. What else influences local district actions?

Public education is a 423 billion dollar business (National School Boards Association, pg. 2). As previously stated, not all of these funds come from local district taxes. While states provide varying levels of funding to their local districts, the federal government also supplies monies to supplement local district budgets. Article 1 Section 8 of the Constitution states that Congress has the power to provide for the general welfare of the country. This has led to court approval of the concept that acceptance of federal grants requires states and districts to follow the federal mandates imposed by the grants (Menacker, pg. 17). General funding of public education is under the jurisdiction of the states, and if they so choose, local school districts within the states. Federal funding is provided to supplement these funds, but not in the realm of general support. Federal support is aimed at the specific directives of the federal legislation that underlies the funding.

Federal and State Requirements

The role of CTE in preparing our national workforce is so significant that it is protected and guided by the specific directives of federal legislation (Camp, et. al., pg. 19). The Smith-Hughes Act of 1917 marked the beginning of federal financial support for secondary CTE in public schools. It also marked the beginning of federal requirements for secondary career and technical education in public schools. Curricula was developed and monitored by the states, but to receive funding they had to submit their state plan for approval at the federal level (Finch and Crunkilton, pg. 15). This act marked the beginning of combined state and federal requirements for CTE.

The Carl D. Perkins Career and Technical Education Improvement Act of 2006 (Perkins IV) embodied a continuation of Federal legislative initiatives channeling funding to CTE. At its inception, Perkins IV funding represented about 1.3 billion dollars for CTE to support upgrades, innovation, expansion, and access. This bill also permitted the continuation of funding to support career and technical student organizations. In the definitions section, the law also defined the term "career and technical student organization" as:

> *"an organization for individuals enrolled in a career and technical education program that engages in career and technical education activities as an integral part of the instructional program."* (Perkins IV, pg. 4)

At the very least, this definition assumes that CTSOs will be integrated into career and technical instructional programs. Many interpret this definition as mandating that CTSOs must be embedded into CTE programs. Perkins IV funding is administered by and initially distributed to local education agencies in each state through their state-level education agency (or department).

Each state agency was still required to write their own State Plan for Career and Technical Education to be eligible to receive Perkins IV funding. State Plans are individualized, but they must adhere to federal legislation in order to be approved. That translates into state-mandated CTSO integration in CTE programs. States could reaffirm this infusion of CTSOs into the curriculum, or they could bolster the requirement for career and technical student organizations in their State Plan. They could also require local education agencies that apply for Perkins funds to assure their participation in CTSOs. This requirement could also be part of a state approval process to operate existing CTE programs or to establish new programs. This requirement could also be part of any request for state funds.

Perkins IV specifically permits career and technical student organizations to receive federal funding to support activities at the state and local levels. In some cases, states may set aside an extra state or federal funding to subsidize career and technical student organization activities. Using leadership and administrative funds available to state education agencies, states may sponsor the part of the salary of one or more state staff. The staff member(s) may be full-time or part-time employees, although full-time employees may have other assigned duties. Other state CTSO funds may be collected through membership dues and/or activity fees. Using these funds, CTSOs have the responsibility to help states meet the challenges set forth in Perkins (ACTE 2006, pg. 7).

Local Requirements

Local education agencies, such as school districts, could have policies and/or procedures that reinforce requirements for career and technical student organization participation in their programs. This could be in response to regulations, or it could just be a strategy for maintaining and/or increasing the quality of local career and technical education programs. A requirement might even exist at the individual school level. Some schools might emphasize CTSOs more than others. Requirements might vary at the school administrative level with some administrators favoring CTSOs more than others.

Districts and/or schools might also set aside part of their CTE funding specifically to support CTSO student activities. Many programs conduct fund raising drives to provide a base of support for these activities. Some programs are able to produce a saleable product to supplement the cost of their CTSO activities. Some schools even hold schoolwide fundraising activities.

Teachers should strive to learn the source of any regulations and/or policies relating to career and technical organizations in their state, their local district, and their school. Sources of information could be school administrators, State Department of Education supervisors, and State Directors or State Advisors for career and technical student organizations. Some regulations and policies may be difficult to discover, because this component of student education may have been in place so long that memory of its origin has faded.

Rules and regulations for more recent initiatives may be more accessible. Although regulations for CTE may be updated periodically and may be considered current between updates, they are often slight modifications to existing initiatives. Gearing up to meet these slight modifications may not be as drastic to school personnel as preparing to meet completely new initiatives of a brand new program.

It may take a little more digging to find CTE and CTSO mandates, but they usually exist in some form. An example of the digging needed to find mention of CTSOs may be found in the High Schools That Work (HSTW) initiative of the Southern Regional Education Board (SREB). Camp, Jackson, Buser, and Baldwin bemoaned the fact that HSTW's push for reforming CTE curriculum to better prepare CTE students for college success does not address CTSOs in their proposed new high school (Camp, et. al., pg. 19). While CTSOs are not one of the key practices of this program, they are briefly mentioned in HSTW's book *Making High Schools Work*. CTSO activities are mentioned as one of the meaningful homework assignments in the chapter "Raising Expectations" (Bottoms, Presson, and Johnson, pg. 42). While this example does not show a direct connection, it does show a connection. There are much stronger connections in federal legislation, and there may also be stronger connections in school, district, or state regulations and procedures.

Many schools have teacher regulation and procedure pamphlets or manuals. A copy of these school or district rules for teachers is usually available upon request to the school administration. These school documents do not always address CTE specifically, but a district policy may be in effect. Many school districts maintain a board policy manual, which is an accumulation of current directives as well as less recent directives that are still in effect. The high school administration should have access to the document, either in print or online. Teachers may not be able to get their own copy, but they should be allowed to view the policy manual. State agencies usually have regulations and/or education policies. Increasingly, these regulations and policies are available online, making them even more accessible.

Resources

The most important feature of career and technical student organizations is not the regulations that exist. CTSOs are more important as a tool than as a rule. When any state or district requires participation in career and technical organizations, the mandate is often intended to infuse the benefits of the CTSO into the curriculum. As an integral part of a career and technical education curriculum, these organizations and their activities are useful tools that can be used to build quality career and technical education programs. CTSOs have the capacity to increase the motivation of students. They can be used to increase the interaction of education and businesses. They can add some element of reality to student learning and practice.

The greatest resource available to facilitate participation in career and technical student organizations is the organizations themselves. They offer curriculum materials that can be used as supplementary and/or embedded activities. These materials provide curricular assistance directed at areas that include but are not limited to:

1. Employability Skills for Students

2. Technical Skills for Students

3. Quality Skills for Students

4. Job Application Skills for Students

5. Leadership Skills for Students

6. Classroom Management for Teachers

These resources can be obtained for a nominal fee; many are included with the price of membership.

Realities

Although the state plan for career and technical education written under federal Perkins legislation may make some mention of CTSOs, a school district and/or school may or may not have specific rules or regulations that require CTSO activity participation. Absence of local mandates regarding CTSOs should not matter. Somewhere in the regulations affecting the program should be a mandate that implies the importance of effective teaching of quality programs. Even without a localized mandate, good teachers create their own need to provide quality instruction for their students. Necessity is the mother of invention in this case; the pioneers of CTSOs invented them because they were needed to accompany and facilitate quality education, not because they were ordered to create them.

Given the well-established co-curricular aspects of CTSOs and the fact that the Perkins definitions refer to them as an integral part of the instructional program, it would be difficult for any enlightened education agency receiving federal funding to ignore the potential benefits of these organizations in their procedures that apply to the support of state CTSO associations and local CTSO chapters. This co-curricular status means that CTSO participation can be considered part of CTE curriculums and programs rather than a program adjunct (Camp, et. al., pg. 42).

Recognized Standards

CTE programs look for recognized standards to support their curriculum goals. One of the focuses of this search is to acquire standards that will be recognized by employers (Grubb, et. al., pg. 76). Many industries have their own trade organizations which may set and/or promote standards, such as the American Welding Society (AWS). Standards may also be set by municipal license testing requirements in areas such as: cosmetology, electrical trades, some health occupations, HVAC, and plumbing.

Sometimes education and industry work together to set standards and even to create curriculum. The National Center for Construction Education and Research (NCCER) has created their Contren® Learning Series to promote standards-based CTE in the construction trades. NCCER also provides tests as an integral part of their curriculum. The National Occupational Competency Testing Institute (NOCTI) tests individuals against nationally recognized standards in such diverse areas as: computers, construction trades, culinary arts, electronics, machining, media, and transportation. NCCER and NOCTI are examples of organizations that bring together educators and industry professionals from across the country to act as a panel of national experts to set curriculum and testing standards for their particular career area.

CTSOs are national organizations that have contest standards in technical and leadership skill areas. They use national experts from education and industry to create and update these contests. CTSO contests are often supported and judged by business and industry experts. The skills that comprise their contests represent national standards that are recognized by these business and industry experts as they support and participate in the competitions. In 2007, SkillsUSA took this one step further as this CTSO started a project to use their contests' national technical committees to develop curriculum standards and test-based occupational credentials as part of their skill contests. Their Work Force

Ready System aims to provide national standards for Skilled and Technical Sciences CTE programs and credentials for students who demonstrate meeting these standards to take to prospective employers.

CTSOs are also recognized nationally in the education arena. In 1999, the U.S. Department of Education under Secretary Richard Riley published their policy that recognized the educational programs and philosophies embraced by vocational and technical student organizations (Camp, et. al., pg. 9-10). In 2006, Dr. Troy Justesen, Assistant Secretary of the U.S. Department of Education's Office of Vocational and Adult Education, sent a letter to colleagues recognizing the following career and technical student organizations:

Business Professionals of America

DECA

Future Business Leaders of America-Phi Beta Lambda

National FFA Organization

Family, Career and Community Leaders of America

Health Occupations Students of America

National Postsecondary Agricultural Student Organization

National Young Farmer Educational Association

Technology Student Association

SkillsUSA

Chapter Five

Enabling Everyone to Win

"Happiness lies in the joy of achievement and the thrill of creative effort."
Franklin D. Roosevelt

Competition

All students should benefit from Career and Technical Student Organization (CTSO) competitive activities. The extra training related to their curriculum, the exposure to the lofty ideals of these organizations, and the opportunity to compete should have a positive impact on every student that participates.

Many of the organizations' activities involve contests. If only the students who win medals at the national level benefit from these activities, then activity efforts were wasted on the other students. If school administrators judge the quality of their career and technical programs on how many state medals the program generates, then the teacher and the program may have been inappropriately judged.

The most vital element of judging is how the students judge themselves. Students need to learn that the joy of achievement does not necessarily mean winning a medal. Learning, growing, and attempting personal best efforts may be the most significant element of competition that the teacher-advisor will see from a group of students. It is the teacher's job to enable the students to understand the essential aspects of competing so that they will not be disappointed by their creative efforts. This is a tough job that requires a huge proactive effort with constant reinforcement before and after the competition.

Although no teacher-advisor can fully manipulate how the students will feel if they don't win a medal, good teachers can coach their students to help them put any disappointment in the proper perspective and minimize or even eliminate its potentially negative impact. Teacher-advisors must be ready to proactively deal with this aspect of competition before signing up any students. Teachers who are not ready to proactively deal with this side of competition may do their students more harm than good by signing them up.

There are many levels that can lead up to a national contest. These vary according to program, school, and state. All programs should have local contests before sending students to the next level contest. Some schools have schoolwide contests before sending students to regional or state contests. School districts may even have district-wide contests. Some states have regional contests that send winning students to their state contests. All states have state level contests before sending students to national contests. If more contests are available, more students get to participate. If more contests are available, participating students become better prepared. More contests also mean more opportunities for students to win medals.

All students can't win medals at all levels, but well-prepared students are more comfortable during the contest. They also feel better about their performance if they are ready to do their best. Well-prepared students usually impress the judges. Judges from the business community usually value all of the students who do a good job in the contest; this can happen during the contest as well as when students mention participating in their career and technical student organization during a job interview. If judges see the whole group of students performing well, they are impressed with the career and technical education programs that provided competitors. It is not unusual for judges to be so impressed with the whole group of students that they score the competitors very closely.

What can teachers do to help make the contest situation a win-win situation for themselves and the students? There are a few issues that they will need to address:

1. Prepare the students' awareness of the true significance of participating in the competition well before the contest.

2. Teach the necessary skills before the contest.

3. Teach the students to understand how to be a personal winner.

4. Assist the students in practicing their skills before the contest.

5. Learn as much as possible about the process of operating the competition.

6. Review contest rules with the students.

7. Assist in maintaining a realistic level of contest quality.

8. Recognize the students for participation and effort, regardless of outcomes.

9. Understand the process of operating a competition, and thereby gain perspective on a realistic expectation of contest quality.

10. Assist contest officials (if needed) in maintaining a realistic level of contest quality for upcoming contests.

Student Preparation

Contests can challenge students to deal with any or all of the following, potentially stressful elements:

1. Unfamiliar setting

2. New equipment

3. Limited time frame

4. Unseen projects

5. An audience

6. Judges appraising each detail of their every move

7. Possible mistakes

8. Complicated directions

9. High-stakes activity

There may be other potentially stressful factors besides these. Students need to be well-prepared to deal with these factors; remember, this should be a positive experience for competing students. How can teachers help to make this a good memory for their students?

Even if teachers know exactly what will be required for an upcoming contest, they should not reveal the details to their students. They can, however, review what has happened at previous contests. If students who competed in a previous contest are available, it is very helpful to have them assist in explaining what new competitors should expect. The student-to-student perspective can be very beneficial.

Contests almost always have a set of general guidelines that are used each year. Occasionally, some students are frustrated by doing a great job at a contest only to find out too late that they violated some rule or procedure that keeps them out of medal contention. Students should get a copy of these guidelines that they can keep. Teacher-advisors should explain and review the meaning of each facet of the contest guidelines with the competitors. This should happen more than once during the preparation process.

If the guidelines are for the national level contest, they may not always be followed exactly at lower level contests. Sometimes these contests do not have the time or resources to exactly duplicate the conditions of a national level contest. In this case, students need to know the different situations that they will face. A compare and contrast teaching model can be useful in gaining student understanding of both situations.

Students also need to know what to bring to a contest. They may need to prepare certain items before the competition. They may need to bring other items, such as tools, to a contest. Students also need to know the dress requirements for the contest. Appropriate appearance is always a factor in the impression that students make on the judges; it is often included in the scoring process as well.

One of the most important preparations that students can receive is quality instruction taught using appropriate standards. Quality career and technical education programs use suitable local, state, and national standards to develop, update, and improve their curriculums. These programs find that many of the skills in the contest are embedded in their curriculum; others may be added to provide instructional enhancement for competing students. This provides foundation skills for competing students, but it does not always simulate contest conditions. How can these conditions be simulated?

Practice, Practice, Practice

When skills are embedded in the curriculum, many opportunities to simulate contest conditions exist. Tests on subsets of skills can use contest guidelines to simulate subsections of contests. Periodic reviews of previously learned large skill sets may be able to duplicate multiple subsections of contests.

Local program contests can be useful for selecting competitors for the next level contest, but they can do more. Reviews preceding these contests offer many preparation opportunities. Once prepared, the local program contests can come very close to duplicating the conditions of an actual contest; this can especially occur if contest guidelines are followed and outside judges are used. These contests also offer opportunities for student recognition. Students will be under a lot of pressure during contests. Practicing can help them to perform well under pressure.

Recognition

When students compete in career and technical student organization contests, all of the students can't win medals. If properly prepared and practiced, all of the students can do an outstanding job of representing themselves, their career and technical education program, and their school. All participants should receive recognition for good performance.

Recognition should always take the form of high praise from the teacher, but there are other forms of recognition that might be possible. How a teacher chooses to recognize his or her students depends on their personal style, the time available, and the availability of other resources. Teachers should never be limited by the perception that students won't like one form of recognition or another. If the form of recognition can be made to fit the teacher's style, it will be easier for the teacher to sell it. If the teacher can positively sell it, the students will probably buy it.

One simple but effective method of recognition is praise from the judges. If judges from the business and/or other important communities tell the students that they are impressed with the performance of all students and that the scores are very close, that is high praise from a respected source. This should be encouraged to happen immediately following the contest. Judges may not realize how important this praise can be to the competitors, but a knowledgeable educator at the contest can request that the judges take this step. Teacher praise can then piggyback on this concept by reminding students how proud they were when the judges gave this praise to their students.

Teachers can also create a "Wall of Fame" in their classrooms where they list all students who "performed at the level of excellence" in their contest. Certificates can be easily printed using one of the many available computer programs. Prizes can be solicited from local company donors (they like to give small items sporting the company name and logo). If the contest is a local or school level contest, teachers may know the scores that students earned in different sections or categories of the contest. This creates the possibility of awarding certificates or prizes to 1st, 2nd, or 3rd place winners in each area.

Many of the official medal suppliers for career and technical student organizations have smaller versions of state and national contest medals for sale. At the local or school level, Gold Medals could be awarded to all students who qualify to move up to the next level. Silver Medals could be awarded to all students who are selected as alternates for the next level contest. Students who win medals should be encouraged to wear them the next school day after receiving their medals. Students should also be encouraged to wear local, regional, state, and/or national medals with their cap and gown at graduation.

Awards ceremonies can be important. Program or school level ceremonies can be used to provide recognition to all students who "performed well". When possible, awards should be given for "performance" rather than for "participation". Performance is a higher level of recognition than participation. Awards ceremonies at the regional, state, or national level can encourage students who will be able to participate next year; even students who don't receive medals at that level can be inspired to come back with more dedication the following year.

Many schools use their public address systems to announce the results of sporting events to the school during morning announcements. This can be used to announce any winners of local contests. It can also be used to congratulate all participants in a contest at any level: school, district, regional, state, or national. Announcements can also be used to reinforce the idea that all of these students have represented their school and their program well.

Personal Best

There should be no losers in competitive career and technical student organization activities. This includes both teachers and students. If properly equipped to compete, students should feel good about their performance. Properly prepared and practiced students should also make the teacher feel well-represented. Medals are nice, but students and teachers don't have to bring back medals to be winners.

This may fly in the face of typical media coverage of competitive events. Usually the media divide competitors into two groups after the event: winners and losers. Trying to determine whether society reflects the media or the media reflects society could be the subject of several books. One thing is clear. Teachers will have to make an aggressive effort to ensure that all of their competitors feel like winners after the competition and awards have ended. It will be extremely difficult for students who do not win medals to be winners unless a proactive teacher-advisor enables their positive outlook in advance and incessantly facilitates their feelings of success.

Prepared and practiced students are capable of demonstrating the good work that the teacher has done both teaching the students and preparing them for a contest. These students often go to an unfamiliar setting, are usually rushed for time to compete, have at least some experts watching and judging their every move, and should feel that this is a high-stakes activity. In spite of the fact that stresses make it difficult to do their best work, they all usually impress the judges with their poise and their skills. How can anyone call any of these students anything less than winners? In this situation, teachers should not have to fake being very proud of their students!

Students, however, often set very lofty goals for themselves. Students have been known to be disappointed for only winning second place in a national CTSO competition. This is like having the winning numbers on your ticket for a $200 million lottery, and then being disappointed to learn that someone else also had the winning numbers so that you only get $100 million for yourself. Teachers additionally need to help put winning in perspective for their students so that the students won't experience a loss when they are actually winning!

Students need to hear about the business and industry employment successes of their predecessors who performed well at previous contests, but did not get a medal. Teacher-advisors may have some of these stories that they can tell to their students. Students need to understand that preparing, practicing, and participating in CTSO competitive activities can play a significant part in their training without worrying about winning medals. Medals are nice, but medals are not necessary for future career success.

There is always the possibility that a small minority of students will not perform as hoped. This can happen for various reasons, but it should always be analyzed from the perspective of a learning opportunity. Although they will want to correct any defects in performance, teachers should take care not to discourage any underperforming student or any audience of potential future competitors. Some good elements can usually be found in any performance. If nothing else, stepping up to enter the competition is a positive act. If an underperforming student is graduating and will not be able to compete again, lessons learned can help the student be better prepared for future, real-life situations. If an underperforming student is not graduating, the student can try again next year. Either way, the benefits of career and technical organizations can apply to all students, regardless of their individual performance levels.

It is important that teachers genuinely feel proud of their students and that they make this known to their students. Administrators should also join in the awareness that these students have proudly demonstrated the quality of their education by performing very well in a CTSO competitive activity. Asking administrators to join in any recognition ceremonies may be a useful way to get them on board with this concept. Their participation serves the teacher as an opportunity to help administrators understand that they should not judge any successful program's participation in these contests only by the number of 1st, 2nd, and/or 3rd place awards that students receive.

Holding a Local Contest

The best way to understand the dynamics of organizing and running a competition is to become involved. The greatest opportunity for involvement is at the local or school level. Teachers may even be able to chair their local or school career and technical student organization competitive activity.

One of the first things to do is to review the national contest. A review of the written contest guidelines is a great start. Some organizations occasionally issue copies of the details of recent national contests; these particulars may be available online, or teachers can contact their state CTSO advisor or state CTSO director for information on the availability of copies of this information. If these copies are not available, it may help to consult with someone who has viewed a recent contest at a higher level.

After sorting through available information, contest coordinators must decide which parts of the contest are possible to do for their contest. Time, materials, sponsorship, equipment, space, and the availability of judges must be considered. Then the actual contest details must be planned and implemented.

Judges need to be obtained and oriented to fairly score students. It should be emphasized that the important thing is to be as equitable as possible when determining scores; each student needs to be judged according to contest standards. Due to time limitations for volunteer judges, orientation usually has to occur on the contest day in the brief time period before the contest starts. The contest chair can give these judges all of the rules and regulations from national guidelines and hope that they will be able to completely understand and memorize the details. The chair can also explain any differences between national guidelines and details in your local contest. This will probably occur simultaneously with getting the rest of the contest ready.

Judge orientation can become easier in later years of the contest if the same judges return each year. With a typical time frame of a year between contests, memories may still have to be refreshed. It must also be understood that if this contest is judged one day each year, judges with ten years of experience actually have only ten days of experience. In spite of these obstacles, judges must be prepared as well as possible. The performance of the students will be similar in many cases. Even judges who try to be perfectly objective will have some of the human factor of individual judgment reflected in their scores. Contest coordinators must do the best that they can, but they will come to realize that absolute perfection is not possible.

Professional baseball offers a good illustration of the human judgment factor in action. Professional umpires are well-trained and experienced. The strike zone is clearly defined in the rules, and they have memorized the rules. Each baseball season these umpires judge the placement of hundreds of pitches. Each pitch is judged well, but the human factor prevents the perfect appraisal of every pitch. Different professional umpires may at times have slightly different strike zones, and there are many pitches that test the edge of the strike zone. Some pitches come in a straight line, but they come pretty fast. Other pitches may dip, rise, or otherwise curve just before entering the strike zone. Professional umpires usually do a good job, but both teams' players seldom agree with all of their calls. Contest management may occasionally have harsh criticisms of the judgments that these umpires make too.

Quality and Reality

Anyone who is deeply involved in the operation of a contest will want to plan for a high-quality contest beforehand. They will strive to keep quality high during the contest. They will also want to appraise the various elements of the contest after completion to keep quality at a high level and/or to improve quality for the next contest that they plan.

Contest chairs or coordinators may get comments from observers of the contest. Observers should take care to be factual and polite. Comments should be made to the chair or coordinator, not to the judges. If judges receive critical comments, they may not volunteer again. Chairs or coordinators need to insulate judges from comments. Further, contest management needs to hear all comments. The contest managers are responsible for planning the next contest and deciding which, if any, changes should be made.

It is impossible for contest management to control how comments are given to them. Sometimes they can be proactive and speak to observers before any comments are given. This will afford the opportunity to explain that nitpicking is not welcome, attempting to come up with a different set of winners after the contest has run is impossible, and only reasonable suggestions for improvement of the next contest will be considered.

If the proactive approach is not feasible, contest management must try to react properly to comments in an effort to set the proper tone. It will be more difficult, but still important, to explain what types of comments are proper. These explanations will also be good to remember if a chair or coordinator goes to another contest where he or she is an observer.

Comments should always be constructive, not destructive. Observers need to understand that once the contest has been completed, improvements should be for the next contest; they should not attempt to ask contest managers to rerun the contest that was already held. Students are not the only ones being scrutinized by judges that often represent business and industry. Observers can undermine the perceived quality of a program if they are not as professional as the students are expected to be.

If the person making the comments is upset or angry, he or she should not make comments in an emotional state. Comments should be made in a calm, professional manner. Adult contest participants and observers should remember that students are present and that the adults should consistently model desired student behavior. More importantly, it is the main job of the teacher-advisors to be putting on a positive face in front of the students so that the students will be as positive as possible. If students see that a teacher is upset about a contest, it can ruin months of proactive student preparation for a positive experience.

Comments should also be based on fact, not emotion. There will be sufficient time for an upset observer to make comments before the next contest. This should allow ample time for an upset observer to regain his or her composure before making comments. This should also allow plenty of time to the observer to review contest rules and carefully decide if comments are highly appropriate. No unreasonable demands should be made of contest management.

If someone has multiple improvement observations, they may need to prioritize their comments. Too many comments may overwhelm contest managers. Too many comments can sometimes be confused with criticisms based more on emotion than fact. Observers should also be told that their comments will be considered, but others may have comments later; every suggestion cannot always be incorporated into the next contest.

Some contest coordinators turn reasonable commentators into volunteers. They invite the adults who have legitimate suggestions to join in the preparation and operation of the contest as a method for the commentators to implement their suggestions for maintaining and/or improving contest quality. This tactic can generate multiple benefits such as:

1. Gaining more assistance for operating the contest

2. Getting the improvements implemented by someone who fully understands the details

3. Letting perfectionists attempt to implement perfection

4. Letting perfectionists learn the compromises of contests

Observers should know that contest quality is not improved by destructive efforts. Only positive efforts directed toward building a quality contest and consistency in the retention and continued training/experience of contest personnel can provide the structure for a better contest.

Importance of Local Contests

Local contests benefit students in many ways. For the student spectator, these contests can generate interest in participation. Having student spectators is a reality for multiyear programs, where students at the early level have not progressed far enough through their CTE program to compete in a local contest. For student participants, these contests offer an opportunity to achieve recognition for their efforts. The result of that effort may be finishing at the top for the overall contest. The result may be performing well without finishing in one of the top spots. Either result can be an effective motivator if the advisor actively praises the students' performance and provides a certificate or some other form of recognition. At this level, the local advisor should even be able to look at scores based on the sections of the contest and provide recognition for these sections.

Local contests also provide more of a safe haven for competition. Students will be nervous, but they should be less nervous than they would be if the contest was held at a higher level. This helps students who finish at the top to be more comfortable if they participate in contests held at a higher level. This level of comfort will help students to feel more prepared for higher level competitions, which can help them to feel better about their performance regardless of the outcome.

Local contests provide more opportunities for students to participate. Although the guidance of the advisor is always the key to how students view the outcome of their performance in a contest, they must be able to participate in order to open up the possibilities for reward and recognition. While the opportunities for recognition are available at many performance levels, students cannot be recognized for non-participation.

The costs of a local contest can be controlled more closely. Keeping registration fees low or eliminating fees altogether can also enable more students to participate. Advisors can limit the expendable materials that are needed. No travel costs should be required. Advisors can solicit donations of any expendable materials that must be used to run the contest from local business representatives.

Local chapters can also raise funds to support contest costs, including the costs of local contests. Another benefit of conducting a local contest to determine which students move on to the next level is that students usually don't mind using monies from local fund raisers to finance registrations and costs for higher level contests if every student has a chance to participate and possibly move up.

Quality of Life Issues

In his book, *The Seven Habits of Highly Effective People,* Stephen Covey tells us that one of the basic tasks of leadership is to improve the quality of life for all stakeholders (Covey, pg. 217). Good teachers strive to be highly effective in order to assist in the education of their students. If their students are better educated, it follows that they should achieve a higher quality of life. When CTE is brought into the education menu, that higher quality of life can include higher earnings. Helping more of their students to participate and to be successful, or even win, at CTSO contests will assist in bringing the potential benefits of CTSOs to their students.

Helping students to learn to put a positive spin on contest outcomes will help them to develop a positive attitude that will enable them to correctly deal with situations that can arise in the workplace. For example, an employee may miss a desired promotion the first time; however, if that employee can still maintain a positive outlook, he or she may get a future promotion. These leadership tasks can be viewed from the long-term perspective of quality of life that educators often stress to their students.

Why wait for this improvement? Helping students compete and feel like winners can improve the quality of life for students while they are still in school. The increased interest and motivation from this spark can ignite the students' educational experience. Improving the students' quality of life in the more immediate sense will also improve the quality of life for their advisor. This can improve the quality of life in the classroom which will increase the teacher's job satisfaction in the classroom. These teacher-advisors can then take satisfaction in observing the impact on both the short-term and long-term quality of their students' lives.

CTE teachers have seen the positive effects that their programs can have on students. The reality foundation of these programs can have the effect of increasing student interest. They can stimulate learning by addressing different learning styles. They can awaken other "intelligences". The result of any or all of these positive effects can be to make the students experience high levels of success.

CTSOs are designed to be an important part of CTE programs. When incorporating their activities, teacher-advisors must plan to attempt to continue this pattern of student success. When it comes to directing student participation in CTSO activities, everyone can win. For the sake of the students, it is imperative for advisors to prepare students and activities to try to make each student come out feeling like a winner. Most students will be able to understand their individual success as a result of these activities if the teacher-advisor enables the attitude and vision of all of their students.

When planning a local contest, wise teacher-advisors allow the students of their local chapter to assist with arrangements, set-ups, soliciting judges, thanking judges, locating prizes, etc. If properly presented, students will usually be willing to help out.

Chapter Six

Skills Contests in the Curriculum

"The point is to develop the childlike inclination for play and the childlike desire for recognition and to guide the child over to important fields for society."

Albert Einstein

The Standards Movement

Nearly every state in the country has identified explicit learning goals that are typically known as learning outcomes or content standards (Wiggins and McTighe, pg. 60). Groups of experts have often been formed to pour over academic subject matter to glean the essential knowledge needed for student success. These experts often sit on national, state, and sometimes local panels or committees charged with establishing content standards for a specific area for which they have specialized knowledge.

The movement to establish content standards has accompanied the push for academic testing as part of the No Child Left Behind Act of 2001 (NCLB). The basic idea is that standards should reflect what students need to know, testing should assess how competent students are in using this knowledge, and the curriculum should be designed to teach the information and skills necessary to pass the tests. By passing these high-stakes tests, high school students are believed to demonstrate the abilities needed to succeed in further education and/or the workplace.

These high-stakes tests have facilitated a realignment of academic curriculum to ensure that what is taught reflects the essential knowledge outlined by the content standards. Academic teachers using this curriculum also need to prepare students for the type of assessments that they will face on these high-stakes tests. One method that the teachers can use to prepare their students is to use tests in their classrooms that mimic the high-stakes tests. This practice can be valuable for CTSO activities as well.

Summative and Formative Tests

Classroom tests are often used to give teachers the opportunity to assess student efforts for the purpose of calculating grades. While this type of grading may not have the same significance as high-stakes NCLB-type testing, the grades do have possible consequences. They are part of the assessment scheme used to determine credit and promotion. This type of test is called a <u>summative</u> test. Summative tests are commonly used at the end of a learning period to appraise and permanently score the level of understanding. These tests are usually thought to be an indicator of *how well the student is* ***doing***. Using summative tests that reflect high-stakes testing methods can give teachers a better prediction of how students might perform on this type of information on an NCLB-type test. It can also provide the students with a practice opportunity where they can become more comfortable with the type of testing that they might face in the future.

Another type of testing tool available to teachers is the <u>formative</u> test. To be effective, this type of test should be given during the learning process. The value of these tests is not found in the grading process. The true value of these tests is to provide feedback while the learning process is still active. Formative testing can be used to discover areas that need more clarification and emphasis. Students bring differing levels of understanding to any learning process. Students also learn in different ways and at different speeds. Formative tests can identify gaps in the students' understanding and potential performance on any type of summative test, including super-summative NCLB-type tests. This gives the teacher a chance to adjust instruction to meet the needs of their students.

Formative tests should be used to monitor instruction. Different groups of students will have different instructional needs to raise their level of understanding. While students always bear a certain level of responsibility for absorbing the efforts of their teachers, it is also accurate to think of formative tests as a measure of *how well the teacher is doing*. This type of test can demonstrate the effectiveness of student learning while teachers are still able to modify their influence. If properly used, formative tests can assist in increasing scores on summative tests. Far too often, teachers do not sufficiently utilize formative tests. Sometimes this is because they don't fully understand the concept. Sometimes, this is because they don't have enough testing materials.

Some teachers have the good fortune of being provided with an abundance of testing and review materials. With plenty of materials, it is easy to use some of the materials for formative testing and review without compromising summative tests. If limited testing and review materials are available, there is a possibility that students will be able to just learn the test by using these materials too often without actually mastering the competencies. Not all teachers have the good fortune of being provided with ample testing and review materials. In either case, CTSO tests and contests can be used for formative testing and review without compromising summative testing materials. Effective usage of formative testing can lead to improved student summative test results.

CTE Standards

Career and technical education programs also have standards that drive the curriculum. The standards for these programs were outlined by panels of experts at the national, state, and local level. These advisory committees or advisory councils also meet to update local program standards. Perkins III required local education agencies to involve parents, teachers, businesses, and labor organizations in the planning, development, implementation, and evaluation of CTE programs (Brustein and Mahler, pg. 51).

An initiative at the end of Perkins III by the U.S. Office of Vocational and Adult Education (OVAE) and codified in Perkins IV, will implement state-approved (summative) testing for completion of CTE programs. This should impact standards; by testing against standards, the need to teach standards is reinforced. Perkins IV also continued the requirement for advisory councils or committees.

While local CTE programs must have advisory committees to plan, develop, and implement their programs, these programs often look to some sort of national standards for guidance in the area of standards. Even programs that base their standards on local municipal codes or local licensing often find these local standards are aligned to or based upon national standards. For local advisory committees, developing their own standards independent of national standards would sometimes be the equivalent of reinventing the wheel. To ignore national standards would also be to ignore the expertise of these national panels and the potential value of these standards for students. Many local advisory committees select a set of national standards, where appropriate, for the local CTE program. The committees still retain the authority to modify these standards to reflect a local focus.

CTE advisory councils or committees may have been setting standards long before academic panels were called upon to do so. Advisory committees or advisory councils were not as popular during the very early days of CTE as they are today (Finch and McGough, pg. 160). While it may seem to today's teachers that advisory committees have always existed, the Vocational Amendments of 1968 provided the first national legislative obligation to formally create federal, state, and local advisory councils for the purpose of developing and guiding CTE (Scott and Sarkees-Wircenski, pg.236). That federal influence continues today with Perkins IV.

Competency-based Education

CTE standards may reflect what the students need to learn for an individual class or a complete program of study. Some CTSOs, such as TSA, provide a crosswalk between their standards and their contests (TSA H.S., pg. 8-9). CTSO contests and activities were designed by experts at the national level to be appropriate for their corresponding career areas. SkillsUSA started a program in 2007 to use their contests and technical committees to create standards and standards-based tests.

Specific standards are often referred to as competencies. Many programs advertise themselves as competency-based. A competency reflects the ability to perform using a skill or group of skills. CTE competencies parallel actions that will be used in the workplace. When assessing student performance, teachers should use specific criteria to clarify each aspect of the competency (Finch and Crunkilton, pg. 254). CTSO contests are designed to test student performance of skills needed in the workplace. Specific contests reflect specific competencies. They also include scoring rubrics to analyze each specific aspect of the competency.

Course construction usually starts out with a small group of competencies and adds to these competencies as the students make progress through the course and through higher level courses. Some competencies are ubiquitous; they may be continually practiced as part of more advanced competencies. Other competencies may not easily lend themselves to this "built-in" review, but all competencies need to be reviewed.

A competency is not something that students previously learned and forgot before graduating; a competency is something that the students still know how to do when they graduate. Reviewing previously learned skills using the same curriculum materials over and over again can yield declining effects, as well as loud groans from students. Career and technical student organization contests often test individual competencies or groups of competencies. Preparing students for a contest offers the chance to have students review competencies via a different venue.

Remaining Competent

The level of mastery of a competency also varies. The initial training level could be at a very high level of competence. If students never repeat the use of the competency during training, that level may drop as the skills fade away. What is considered a passing grade for a competency can vary from school to school and even from program to program within a school. For some programs, 85%

mastery could be required for passing the competency while other programs might consider 70% a minimum passing grade. Many other percentages are possible as well. When a competency is used in the workplace, however, the lowest acceptable demonstration of that competency might be 100%.

Again, the initial competency level could be the highest level achieved, if students don't repeatedly use the competency during training. Once students stop practicing the competency, their ability could drop from the initial mastery level. A student who mastered a competency at an 85% level could have his or her mastery drop to 65%. A student who mastered the competency at a 70% level could have his or her mastery drop to 50%. Important competencies should also not be skills that were once known at an acceptable level that have since deteriorated to an unacceptable level.

Finding more opportunities to practice competencies, especially in a new and exciting venue, can help students maintain their skills. It can also give students the opportunity to increase their skills above the initial mastery level. The more important that a competency is to the students' on-the-job future, the more important it becomes for the training program to build in opportunities to practice and increase skills levels for that competency. Giving students a different venue to hone their skills is much more interesting and challenging than simply retesting a competency.

Selecting Contest(s)

Teachers should examine the list of national technical skills contests offered by the career and technical student organization that represents their career and technical program area. Contests whose titles appear to indicate a connection should be considered. When this inexorably happens, a listing of contest guidelines should be obtained and read. While reading, teachers should compare the contest guidelines to the skills taught in their course(s). Any match should be highlighted, and a list of matches should be written for each contest.

Once this research has been completed, teachers can select contests with the most matches for first consideration. A review of course outlines will reveal when these technical skills are taught. They are often scattered throughout the course(s). Teachers will have to look for opportunities to use the contest for review, once all of the contest skills have been covered in their course(s). Some contests will mesh perfectly with the curriculum outline; others might require a reshuffling of curriculum.

Opportunities to Review

The best way to begin is to select at least one skills contest that fits or is close to fitting the curriculum. The contest skills are located in the curriculum, and there is no reason why this review opportunity should not be added to the curriculum. Curriculums using competency-based education lists might also consider embedding CTSO contests in their competency check-off list.

If no contest fits exactly but is highly related to the goals of the career program, some tweaking of the curriculum may be necessary. These contests are usually constructed and adjusted by a panel of national experts in the field; their input can be considered as part of an industry standards and advisory process that can be meshed with a local advisory committee. National career and technical student organization standards can be part of the standards used to build a standards-based career and technical curriculum. Teachers can take any needed changes to their advisory committee for advice, adjustments, and eventual approval.

How this built-in review is used by the teacher may depend upon the application of appropriate timing. The review should occur when it best supports the curriculum. If that time corresponds with the timing for a local contest, shortly preceding the next level contest, then this could become the local contest for the program. If the timing is off, this could become the practice for the local contest which will occur later in the year. Top quality programs may be able to incorporate more than one local contest into their curriculum, which offers students more than one local contest opportunity. In this desired scenario, it would be difficult to time each review to become the local contest.

However the timing occurs, the connection to the career and technical organization should be emphasized. This may necessitate some instruction about the organization itself. The instruction should include information about national, regional, and state contests. It should also include information about the local contests. Even if the review contest is not the actual local contest, the connection to the local contest should be shown to students. If the local contest includes recognition for participants, the motivation that recognition can generate should also be connected. The recognition does not need to be expensive. Printed certificates and/or postings of achievement on a classroom or laboratory wall can serve as motivation. Inexpensive prizes that may often be solicited as donations from industry supporters can be of value as well.

Inspection and Introspection

Scoring rubrics that accompany CTSO contests are valuable in determining winners in a competitive review. They can also be used by students to score each other. High school students are capable of using these rubrics to score their peers. It would not be unethical to allow the students to score each other for the purpose of the contest as long as no formal summative grades were attached. Scoring other students can keep the students active, but it can also have other benefits.

It can help students to analyze the crucial aspects of the competency for other students and for themselves as well. Bonstingl points out that quality systems set clear, attainable expectations for their people at the onset of any endeavor (Bonstingl, pg. 56). Reviewing the scoring rubric beforehand can help students to prepare for the upcoming activity. This can also help students to better inspect their own work during the activity by emphasizing the important details that are necessary to complete a competency activity.

Active participation is an important part of quality instruction (Cummings, pg.154). Students can benefit from the process of making presentations or performing demonstrations, but when the audience of other students just sits passively watching, they are not always paying as much attention as they should. While students score other students during presentations, they are participating more actively. Using a scoring rubric can broaden the understanding of the details that must be followed to develop high performance of a competency. This process has other benefits as well.

Scoring other students helps the students to practice using the rubric. This practice can expand students' understanding of the rubric and its expectations. Scoring other students may also help a student to reflect more deeply on aspects of his or her own performance. This introspection may be more effective than being judged by another. As students look inward, they may gain not only a deeper understanding of the rubric, but they may gain insight into how the teacher and others may view their work. Student appraisal of their own work has been recognized as a valuable aspect of CTE (Giachino and Gallington, pg. 193). Educators often view rubrics as tools that help to increase a teacher's objectivity. They may also help students to view the grading process as a more objective, or fair, process.

When judged by others, especially in a summative situation, the human reaction is to become slightly defensive in interactions with the judge or teacher. While a teacher might hope that a student will use constructive criticism to achieve a higher future score, this may sometimes be at odds with the student's hope that he or she might be able to influence the teacher for a higher score or grade. Having a better understanding of the parameters used for scoring and seeing their own mistakes through the eyes of their teacher might help students understand the importance of correcting these mistakes in the future. Being scored by fellow students in a formative manner puts the use of the rubric in the mode of a non-threatening appraisal. It can also help a student to put his or her mistakes in a better light when they see that other students are making the same mistakes.

Rubric Possibilities

A typical grading situation, without rubrics and without student participation in rubrics, may be viewed as a somewhat arbitrary punishment by the student. It is somewhat arbitrary, because the student lacks the teacher's insight into the parameters of the grading process. It is punishment heavy, because it typically points out only mistakes that the teacher (somewhat arbitrarily) views as mistakes. If it is used for summative grading, it can be perceived as punitive. Psychologists are aware that any possible positive effects of punishment diminish as children grow older and that punishment often creates a negative effect (Kagan and Segal, pg. 174). The proper use of rubrics can help to change this relationship.

Teacher-advisors should be aware that relationships between supervisors and their supervised employees, both in the workplace and in a school setting, are similar in nature. Goldhammer, Anderson, and Krajewski point out that the aim of good school supervision is to create an element of self-supervision for teachers (Goldhammer, Anderson, and Krajewski, pg. 42). Carnevale, Gainer, and Meltzer stress that employees should be trained for self-directed learning (Carnevale, Gainer, and Meltzer, pg. 63). Gaining a more thorough understanding of the parameters of judgment and becoming more proficient at grading their own work can help to train students for more success in the workplace. Providing formative opportunities enables students to correct their mistakes well in advance of the permanence of a summative judgment.

Once an advisor understands the purpose of scoring rubrics in CTSO contests, he or she can begin to imagine the possibilities of using rubrics in everyday competency-based projects and other educational activities. It bears repeating that teachers, not students, bear final responsibility for grading summation. Even so, rubrics can be an excellent tool for teachers to use with CTSO and CTE as they assess their students' understanding by using performance applications. Using the application of performance and products in the evaluation process complicates the grading judgment of the teacher, but rubrics can effectively simplify this process (Wiggins and McTighe, pg. 172-189). Rubrics are an effective tool for assessment ((ITEA, pg. 83). Without extensive experience in developing rubrics, teachers would ordinarily look to some other resource for assistance.

CTSOs have already furnished a resource for CTE rubrics. Scoring rubrics are included with their contests. These rubrics are more specific to CTE than some other educational rubric sources. Most, if not all, of the CTSO rubrics are specific to CTE competencies. Even when the CTSO rubric is not a perfect fit, it may provide a base that can be modified for teacher and student usage.

Chapter Seven

CTSO Leadership Contests

"If we want our children to possess the traits of character we most admire, we need to teach them what those traits are and why they deserve both admiration and allegiance."

William Bennett

Are Other Skills Needed?

When CTE teachers look through lists of technical skills contests for a related Career and Technical Student Organization, they usually find at least one highly familiar competitive activity. The relationship of CTSO leadership contests to their specific career and technical education program also exists, but it may be more subtle. CTE teachers who are specialists in the technical skill area that they teach should recognize the importance of sending students into the workforce with these technical skills. Other skills are sometimes classified as attitudes, soft skills, interpersonal skills, employability skills, workplace behaviors, and even affective work competencies. CTSOs often classify these skills as leadership skills. There is no need to search for these skills in CTSO contests if the teacher-advisor doesn't think that they will be needed by their students.

Bloch cites leadership-type skills as needed to keep a job (Bloch, pg. 114). Littrell, Lorenz, and Smith state that an employer expects employees to demonstrate proficiency in job knowledge, job accuracy, and job productivity, but they should also demonstrate leadership skills in these areas:

1. Attitude

2. Attendance

3. Cooperation

4. Courtesy

5. Honesty

6. Initiative

7. Loyalty

8. Performance

9. Professional Appearance

10. Punctuality

(Littrell, Lorenz, and Smith, pg. 29-36)

Boyett and Conn speculate that work unit teams and self-managed teams will be an essential element of the 21st Century workforce (Boyett and Conn, pg. 237). These opinions are expressed by reputable persons with knowledge in this area, but is there more evidence to support the importance of leadership skills? Two reports that resulted from U.S. Department of Labor initiatives are most often cited to represent the need for teaching skills other than academic and technical skills: ASTD and SCANS (Scott and Sarkees-Wircenski, pg. 9).

ASTD

The American Society for Training and Development (ASTD) is an association of industry, government, education, and research professionals with a common interest in human resources. In 1986, the U.S. Department of Labor provided a grant to enable this group of professionals to research what employers were coming to expect from their employees. ASTD's researchers found that employers wanted more than the basic four skills:

1. reading

2. writing

3. computation

4. problem-solving

While these skills were considered important to the success of their organizations, employers also wanted their employees to have these equally important skills:

A. communication (oral and listening)

B. personal management (self-esteem, motivation, and employability)

C. group effectiveness (interpersonal skills, negotiation, and teamwork)

D. influence (organizational effectiveness and leadership)

(Carnevale, Gainer, and Meltzer, pg. 17-36)

Secretary's Commission on Achieving Necessary Skills (SCANS)

In 1990 the U.S. Secretary of Labor's Commission on Achieving Necessary Skills was asked to examine the demands of the workplace and to advise the Secretary about the skills needed to successfully enter employment. Their report was issued in 1991 (SCANS, pg. xiii). The SCANS report determined that three foundational skills and five workplace competencies were needed for effective job performance (Scott and Sarkees-Wircenski, pg. 10).

The three foundation skills outlined by SCANS are:

1. Basic Skills

2. Thinking Skills

3. Personal Qualities

These basic skills include communication abilities such as speaking and listening. Thinking skills include problem-solving abilities. Personal qualities are responsibility, self-esteem, self-management, sociability, and integrity (SCANS, pg. 16).

The commission's report also identified five competencies that they proposed to be the foundation of the modern workplace dedicated to excellence:

1. Resources

2. Interpersonal

3. Information

4. Systems

5. Technology

The commission also proposed that the acquisition of these competencies must begin in the schools. Two of these competencies refer to the use of resources and ability in technology. Three of these competencies have sections that relate directly to leadership:

1. Interpersonal (teamwork, service, and leadership)

2. Information (communication)

3. Systems (social and organizational)

Members of SCANS believed that these competencies (including leadership-type abilities) apply to every level of the modern quality organization (SCANS, pg. 11-13).

While ASTD and SCANS initiatives date back to the 20th Century, a 2005 survey (previously mentioned in Chapter One) from The Manufacturing Institute reaffirmed the importance of employability skill sets. Basic Employability Skills was the most desired set of attributes cited by employers in this 21st Century survey.

CTSO Opportunities

Student organizations are known to offer opportunities for students to gain leadership experience (Littrell, Lorenz, and Smith, pg. 124). CTSOs can be utilized to offer training and practice experiences within the relatively safe confines of the career and technical education program. All students can be involved in learning some aspects of leadership by participating in CTSO leadership activities. While some of these activities clearly involve leading and some of these activities clearly involve following, many of these activities involve both aspects of these essential employment skills.

CTSOs have also organized competitive leadership activities. These individual contests often have similar names and goals. The fact that these similar leadership contests are found in so many CTSOs could be the result of copying an original idea to avoid the invention process. These organizations were developed at different times, not all at once. We know that people have copied, expanded, and improved ideas throughout history. Regardless of their origin, good ideas tend to survive the test of time.

Whereas technical skills activities are more specific to the experience, education, and/or training of particular career and technical education areas, leadership skill activities are more ambiguous. This situation creates the opportunity for CTE teachers to partner with or otherwise involve any receptive academic subject teachers. Moreover, some academic teachers may be willing to undertake coordination of a contest themselves. Others may just be willing to judge at a local or school level. One way to tempt their involvement is to ask their advice on any related contest to insure that student work on the contest meets the academic standards for their area. This possibility is enhanced when academic and career/technical teachers share common students, and it can be extended to include any academic integration into the career and technical curriculum.

Some competitive leadership activities involve individual students, but other activities involve teams of students. An examination of student benefits for individual students must investigate the skills that have been prepared and practiced. This can be done for team events as well, but team events always offer the opportunity for students to learn how to interact as part of a team. Initially, this can seem confusing if students experience learning pains in their attempt to form-up as a team. Once students begin to function as a team, the teamwork-learning benefits of this type of activity begin to appear. Once students begin to function well as a team, the teamwork-learning benefits of this type of activity actually become clear.

Public Speaking

There are several competitive CTSO activities that utilize communication skills. One type of communication contest is the pre-written and practiced speech, where students work on a known subject in advance of the contest. The speech is first outlined and written. It should contain all of the elements of good, language arts-based communication. The speech should be practiced and at least semi-memorized. (Note cards may be allowed.) Poise, posture, voice projection, pronunciation, speech organization, and quality are among the elements that students should prepare to have scored by the judges. These contests usually just involve speaking, but some also include electronic or other visual enhancement. The exact judging criteria will vary from organization to organization, but the ideas are highly related. In fact, the names of these contests are also similar:

CTSO	Contest Name
BPA	Prepared Speech
HOSA	Prepared Speaking
HOSA	Researched Persuasive Speaking
FCCLA	Illustrated Talk

FCCLA	Interpersonal Communications
FFA	Prepared Speaking
SkillsUSA	Prepared Speech
TSA	Prepared Presentation

Career and Technical Student Organizations also have speaking contests where students do not arrive with pre-written and pre-practiced speeches. These contests usually give students a topic at the contest. Students are then given a prescribed amount of time to prepare a speech on that topic. This limited amount of time also includes any practice time. Then the students present their speeches to the judges. Not every organization has this contest. For the CTSOs that do have this contest, the exact judging criteria and use of presentation visuals will vary from organization to organization, but the basic ideas are analogous. The names of these contests are also comparable:

CTSO	Contest Name
BPA	Extemporaneous Speech
HOSA	Extemporaneous Speaking
FFA	Extemporaneous Speaking
SkillsUSA	Extemporaneous Speaking
TSA	Extemporaneous Presentation

Written Communications

Communication skills are important at many levels. Many Career and Technical Student Organizations include competitive activities that involve writing skills. These may or may not involve an oral presentation of the written document(s). They also may include pictures, drawings, or graphs. This category of activity usually involves the writing and other construction of some sort of booklet, manual, portfolio, pamphlet, etc.; therefore, it will be referred to here as the manual category. The activities in this category are often centered on the theme of the manual, and the names of the individual contests often reflect this theme:

CTSO	Contest Name
DECA	Civic Consciousness Project
DECA	Creative Marketing Project
DECA	Free Enterprise Project
DECA	Learn and Earn Project
DECA	Public Relations Project

Chapter Seven – CTSO Leadership Contests

FFA	National Chapter Award
SkillsUSA	American Spirit
SkillsUSA	Community Service
SkillsUSA	Health Occupations Professional Portfolio
SkillsUSA	Occupational Health and Safety
SkillsUSA	Outstanding Chapter
TSA	Desktop Publishing
TSA	Engineering Design
TSA	Technical Research and Report Writing

Job Interview

Another competitive activity that is common to some CTSOs is the employment interview contest. The competitive activities used may include preparing a resume, filling out a job application, interacting with office personnel before the interview, and playing the part of an applicant in front of an interview panel. Preparing for this activity is excellent practice, both for the contest and for future real-life interviews. This contest easily demonstrates the connection between CTSO leadership activities and preparation for future employment success. Not every CTSO has one of these activities in their repertoire, but many do. The contest guidelines and judging criteria will be somewhat analogous, as are the names:

CTSO	Contest Name
BPA	Interview Skills
HOSA	Interviewing Skills
FCCLA	Job Interview
FFA	Job Interview
SkillsUSA	Job Interview

Meeting Etiquette

Preparing students to function properly in a formal meeting using a current version of *Roberts Rules of Order* is another useful leadership skill for students. At first glance, parliamentary procedure may seem to have more civic ties than industry ties, but communication skills are used in the workplace every day. Sometimes they duplicate part or all of these particular meeting skills. These skills are also useful when holding formal meetings for a CTSO local chapter. Knowledge of these skills can also

50   Dale R. Derrickson, Ed.D.

make students more confident to run for a school, regional, state, and/or national CTSO office. Competitive activities using formal meeting skills are:

CTSO	Contest Name
BPA	Parliamentary Procedure Team
HOSA	Parliamentary Procedure
FCCLA	Parliamentary Procedure
FFA	Parliamentary Procedure
SkillsUSA	Chapter Business
TSA	Chapter Team

General Knowledge

Competitive activities exist that test students regarding career and technical knowledge, current events, math, science, knowledge of their CTSO, etc. These activities situate teams of students in a game show style event where points are earned for each correct answer. Some contests have set points; other contests have students bid on the points for each question. Most of these competitions are general to a specific CTSO, but at least one of them is specific to a defined career area within a CTSO:

CTSO	Contest Name
DECA	DECA Quiz Bowl
HOSA	HOSA Bowl
SkillsUSA	Health Knowledge Bowl
SkillsUSA	Quiz Bowl
TSA	Technology Bowl

Ceremonial Presentations

Some leadership activities are related to individual traditions of the CTSO. These activities emphasize communication skills for students in the contests. For students who would rather read a script than write their own speech, these contests may be their ticket to prepare and practice their communication skills. The FFA contest is a competition for an individual student; it involves giving an oral presentation and answering questions. The SkillsUSA contest is a team event; it involves oral presentations and ceremonial coordination for building an emblem. These contests are:

CTSO	Contest Name .
FFA	Creed Speaking
SkillsUSA	Opening and Closing Ceremonies

Leadership Integration

Can leadership contests be incorporated into the career and technical curriculum? Some of the leadership skills and teamwork skills that these contests enhance should be part of the career and technical curriculum. Individual curriculums will have to be scanned to find which leadership skills are most appropriate as well as when and how these skills can be taught. Once the leadership skills are inserted, skills contests that review, practice, and raise the level of competency for these skills can be examined. Some contests may fit better than others.

If the skills aren't already taught in the curriculum, then one way to get started is to select a contest that seems to offer the most possibilities for usage. The teacher can start by preparing students to compete in a local contest for this activity. Competition helps to bring an early element of reality to the process. Once the teacher has experienced the leadership elements that the contest contains, he or she can look for spots in the curriculum where these elements can be introduced and explained. Once this effort is successful, teachers should look at other leadership contests for possible use.

If leadership elements are already contained in the curriculum, teachers can look for contests that enable a review of these elements. If the fit is not perfect because there are more elements in the contest than in the curriculum, there are two ways to handle this opportunity. Part or parts of the contest may fit well; then only that part might be used for review. If students want to compete in the formal contest, they would have to learn the other part or parts of the contest. Another way to handle this opportunity is to add the parts that aren't presently there to the curriculum. This might expand and enhance the leadership training that is already embedded in the curriculum.

Investment

It may seem like a lot of work to teach non-technical skills. Teaching these non-technical skills may even take some time away from teaching technical skills. It is rare to find a program that has had its time allotment for teaching technical skills expanded. It is not rare to find a technical career that has expanded its technical knowledge base by adding new technologies. Still, there are many good reasons why the effort to teach leadership skills is still worthwhile.

Leadership skills need to be part of the package of employability skills that are important to students' future on-the-job success. Students with good employability skills who have a good foundation of technical skills will usually do well in the workplace; employers are usually willing to teach employees with good leadership skills any extra technical skills that they need these employees to know. Students without good employability skills may not do well on the job; they may even lose their job as a result.

Technical skills are important. Students need technical skills to get a job. They need leadership skills to keep their jobs and advance in their careers. Teaching leadership skills will take effort and time.

Dale R. Derrickson, Ed.D.

Effort and time are precious commodities in CTE classrooms and laboratories. Having established the potential benefits for students, what are the potential benefits for the teacher-advisor?

Return on Investment

The modern workplace has blurred the lines between leaders and followers. Employees may be followers for some activities and leaders in other activities. Employees may progressively find themselves operating as team members. The leadership qualities promoted by CTSOs include aspects of leadership that benefit both students and their teacher-advisor. When students increase their communications skills, the teacher gets to work with stronger communicators. This circumstance provides a higher quality and quantity of necessary feedback for the teacher. When the interpersonal skills of students improve, there are less incidents of discourse for a teacher to manage. When teamwork skills improve, the quality of any group efforts improve. When organization and self-management skills improve, the CTE program can function more like a well-oiled machine.

One essential quality that cannot be overlooked is motivation. Motivated students are easier to teach. Because they are more interested, motivated students are primed to learn more. Because they are not slowed by a lack of motivation, these students learn at an accelerated rate. If CTSO activities were a separate, add-on activity, the time taken to add these activities would be cancelled out by the benefits of motivation. CTSO activities are not add-ons; they mesh completely with the objectives of related, quality CTE programs. Therefore, the time taken in these activities not only makes other facets of the program shine, they completely integrate with existing instructional goals.

Chapter Eight

Leadership Opportunities

"It is always easy to obey, if one dreams of being in command."
Jean-Paul Sartre

Teacher Roles

Teachers will find that their job entails following other leaders and leading students. Opportunities to learn and practice leadership skills have the unique capability to make teachers stronger in both endeavors. It is important that teachers model the behavior of good follower; students may model their behavior on the job upon the observed behavior of their teachers. It is important that teachers constantly practice good leadership; learning is more effective when the students follow the leadership of the teacher.

Teachers will also find that their role often alternates between the duties of a leader and the obligations of a follower. The teacher supervises their classroom, but the teacher reports to a supervisor as well. The teacher's role as a leader is imperative to the success of their classroom, but the teacher's role as a follower is important to the success of the mission of the school. Both of these roles must be accepted and implemented for the teacher to be successful in his or her employment experience.

Student Roles

In today's workplace, it is essential that students learn the art of leadership. They will, of course, need to be good followers. This is especially important when considering the type of jobs available when students first enter the workplace, but students should also learn to lead. In today's workplace, the emphasis on traditional management has changed. The traditional employee-management roles have evolved, and employees often find themselves making more management decisions at work. They may also find themselves in the position of group leader. Some students will be promoted into leadership/management positions at some point in their career.

Students who learn to be good followers and leaders can also demonstrate the traits of more effective students. It is possible that their cooperation with their teacher will improve. Their interaction with their fellow students may improve. Their interest in and understanding of classroom and laboratory activities can be heightened. All of these things can serve to make the educational setting a happier place for teachers and students.

Dale R. Derrickson, Ed.D.

CTSO Opportunities

Career and Technical Student Organizations offer leadership opportunities for students and teachers. The National Coordinating Council for Vocational Student Organizations suggested that a local CTSO chapter is a "leadership laboratory" (NCCVSO, pg. 16). The realm of CTSO leadership opportunity can range far and wide, but it usually starts close to the classroom. The opportunities afforded close to the classroom may also represent the greatest number of opportunities for students and teachers. These opportunities may also represent the greatest need for students. In the history of CTSOs, the first organizations were formed from the local level up based on the need for such programs. Regardless of how the organization was formed, the local level still forms the basis of support for all CTSO activities. Strong local organizations create the only foundation that can support a strong regional, state, and/or national organization.

Teachers can start a local chapter of their CTSO at their school. This type of chapter usually includes their students; sometimes students from other teachers are included to form a multiple-section local chapter. Once any type of associated local chapter is formed, at least one advisor is needed. There can be more than one advisor per chapter if the teachers are available and willing to participate. The opportunity to become an advisor should not be limited to the career and technical teachers; academic teachers that share these students should be offered the opportunity to participate as well. Local CTSOs offer local leadership opportunities for teachers. Teachers can take advantage of this opportunity while remaining close to their home base. The existence of a local chapter can also facilitate the immersion of the CTSO into the teacher's curriculum. The local advisor lays the groundwork for student affiliation and success with the CTSO.

CTSO Resources

Teachers should not have to write the curriculum for forming and operating a local chapter. Most CTSOs can provide the guidelines for starting and running local chapters. The amount of written materials varies according to the organization, but sufficient materials usually exist to assist the teacher with this activity. These materials are often provided by the national offices of the CTSO, although state and regional offices may also have materials available. Posters, guidelines, handbooks, and membership recognition are among the resources offered. Assistance for implementation of activities is always offered at the CTSO's national level. Detailed descriptions of the duties of each officer are also available.

Assistance can usually be found at the state, school district, and school level as well. Each organization typically has a state advisor or state director to coordinate activities at the state level. Districts may have someone coordinating activities at the district level. Schools may have someone in a CTSO leadership role; if not, they may have an experienced teacher who already operates a local chapter. If no one at the school is operating a local chapter, a state or district coordinator should be able to locate someone at a nearby school to assist the teacher. Of course, these coordinators can offer some direction as well.

Membership

As the Chapter Advisor starts to locate and use local chapter guidelines and materials, the advisor will discover that the activities are designed around students. CTSOs are, after all, student organizations. There are many potential benefits for students who can participate in the activities of a local chapter. The first benefit is membership.

Membership brings many things. National CTSOs usually provide membership cards, posters, newsletters, and/or magazines that promote the activities and the ideals of the organization to new members. Membership helps students gain awareness of regional, state, and national competitions, as well as the right to participate in these competitions. One significant benefit of membership is that students gain an understanding of being part of something that is larger than themselves as individuals, that has nationally-recognized objectives, that promotes high standards, that interacts with the business community, and that can bring a new sense of importance to those who belong to the organization. As a member, students should come to understand that they are part of something that extends beyond their classroom. Advisors should assist in this understanding, and they should benefit as leaders and teachers who have students that are motivated by the ideals and activities of their CTSO.

CTSO Leadership Training

A teacher-advisor that is new (or an experienced teacher-advisor that is expanding his or her CTSO horizons) will find numerous resources available from CTSOs to assist them in teaching leadership skills. In addition to these resources, CTSOs also offer their own leadership training for students. This can be a valuable resource.

One version of leadership training is the leadership training institute. In this format, students and their advisor attend a leadership training seminar that is sponsored and operated by the national office of the CTSO. The program that is offered may be for students from across the country, or the programs may be offered on a regional basis. This formal training usually brings in experts to run workshop sessions over a period of several days to train the students in leadership concepts. Training programs may touch on some or all of the following concepts:

1. Business Partnerships

2. Chapter Management

3. Citizenship

4. Community Service

5. Communication

6. Delegating

7. Decision Making

8. Etiquette

9. Leading and Influencing

10. Mentoring

11. Motivating

12. Organizational Functions and Opportunities

13. Planning

14. Parliamentary Procedure

15. Teamwork

These institute-types of leadership training may offer workshops that reach beyond the above list. They usually have a comprehensive approach to leadership. The presentation methods are usually fun for the students. Extra fun activities may also be included to keep the students entertained. Traveling to the location and meeting students from across the country are also high points for students.

While the institute-type of leadership training is extensive, it can also be expensive. Travel, meals, hotel, and institute registration costs can get relatively high. While the value of this type of training program is worth the cost, it can be difficult for a local chapter to come up with the funding every year. If the teacher-advisor can find a way to attend at least once, their exposure to this professional training will help them to better conduct their own training for years to come.

There are many ways to deal with this cost. Corporate sponsorship may be available for at least one year. Raising funds over several years may build up enough to cover the costs. Keeping costs down may be helpful. The advisor can plan for attending when a program is offered closer to home, minimizing travel costs. Limiting the number of students that attend (while getting the advisor there to learn the techniques) may also be helpful. If the state office sends state officers for formal training, an advisor may also access this training by supporting a student who can get elected to a state office and offering to chaperone that same student at the training site. If the advisor's CTSO offers leadership training workshops before, after, or during their national conference, the advisor and students can sign up for these sessions; at the very least, they will already have traveled to the conference location.

State CTSO offices may also offer state and/or regional training. While the state office may not have the same level of resources to conduct training sessions as the national office, state workshops are often modeled after the national leadership training institutes. Some of these training sessions are offered to all officers of local chapters. An advisor may be able to raise the somewhat lower level of funding needed to attend these training programs with their students. Other training sessions may be only for state and/or regional officers. Wise advisors can encourage their students to run for state office and offer to chaperone and/or assist with the state officer team if any of their students are elected to that team.

Workplace Parallels

When teachers are able to help students connect classroom activities to the real world, students become more interested in participation. Career and technical education teachers should look for opportunities to further illustrate how their activities parallel with the world of business and industry. Many professional organizations exist for working professionals. Some of these professionals may take leadership positions in the organization, but mere membership is considered to be a very important part of the working professionals' career. Working professionals use the information disseminated by these organizations to maintain and increase their knowledge and skills. Membership in professional organizations can be highly valued and encouraged by employers. Professionals usually list their membership on job applications and resumes. CTSOs can provide students with their first opportunity to be involved in a professional organization for students. These organizations are often recognized and respected by future employers.

Advisor Leadership

Teacher-advisors have other leadership opportunities within the framework of the CTSO organization. These leadership opportunities can help them to gain further insight and understanding of the potential of the organization for their students. In some circumstances, they may be able to influence the direction of their organization. Some of them may use this experience on their own resumes if they decide to apply for leadership positions in the education field. CTSO national offices are directed by former teacher-advisors who moved up the ladder of their CTSO organization. This ladder offers many leadership opportunities itself. The rungs of this ladder may vary from organization to organization, but the opportunities exist in some form.

In some cases, local chapters may be clustered together by school. Teacher-advisors may wish to form a school council to coordinate and promote the school's CTSO activities. Conducting the business of council can offer further teacher leadership opportunities. It may also be able to broaden and deepen local CTSO activities for students.

Another possible result of this coordination of efforts may facilitate the school's participation in CTSO activities that take place outside of the school. Accompanying students to activities outside of the school offers other opportunities. Chaperones may be needed to guide students at regional, state, and/or national conferences and institutes. Observation of these events can help teacher-advisors to strengthen their students' preparation for local contests. At some CTSO events, especially at the national level, seminars are offered for advisors. These seminars can provide valuable leadership and organizational insights.

CTSOs are student organizations; however, they must receive their guidance and inspiration from adult educators. At many levels, these organizations are operated with teacher-advisor input. Membership on an advisory board, steering committee, or conference committee can represent a valuable leadership opportunity for teachers. Teacher-advisors will discover that interaction with any extra CTSO activity helps them to better understand and utilize the benefits offered by the organization. It also helps them to become better followers and better leaders. Their leadership can be a precious commodity to both students and their fellow educators.

The Local Chapter

Students can also benefit from participating in the leadership activities of a local chapter. A local chapter offers opportunities for more students to occupy the formal offices that are authorized by their

CTSO. Students who have served as president, vice president, secretary, treasurer, etc. of a local chapter can use that experience to run for a state and/or national office. Students who are not elected as officers can take part in discussing and deciding the operations of the local chapter; some can serve on committees that may operate certain activities. All of these experiences are good for students, both during school and after graduation.

The potential exists for local chapters to have many activities. Fund raising to support any activities is important. Participating in CTSO contests at the local and higher levels is another important activity. Local chapters have other potential activities, such as:

1. Promotion of Activities

2. Recruiting New Members

3. Recognition Events for Participants

4. Community Service Projects

5. School Service Projects

6. Business and Industry Speakers

7. Field Trips

8. Sponsorship for Activities

9. Whole Chapter Competitions

Any benefits that national organizations offer can be offered to greater numbers of students at the local level. Activities at the local level support all activities at a higher level. Greater participation in activities leads to greater benefits to both students and teachers. This does not mean that new teachers should jump in and try to do everything simultaneously. Teachers should start slowly and not initially take on more than they can handle. Once these teacher-advisors gain experience and confidence, they should not limit their participation to entry-level exposure. They should look for opportunities to incorporate the next level of benefits available to their students and themselves.

Excellence vs. Complacency

Teacher-advisors should never take on more than they can comfortably handle. However, once they have learned to handle what they have taken on, they should not become too complacent. Too much complacency can be too much lost opportunity. Exploring and understanding the possibilities of CTSO activities should be ongoing; this can lead to increased ability to incorporate the utility of these organizations. They were constructed from the ground up to provide tools for teachers and inspiration for students.

CTSO opportunities can benefit both students and teachers. CTSOs can make the career and technical education program more exciting and meaningful to students. The motivation of students in the program can lead to a more enjoyable and rewarding situation for teachers. The effects can be immediate and long term. This opportunity has the potential to make teachers and students better followers and better leaders while they interact in the classroom and begin to command their future. Many labor and employment experts, including members of SCANS, believe that leadership can and must be taught in schools. In order to do this, schools must provide structured opportunities for students to acquire leadership skills (SCANS, pg. 19).

Local Contest Scenario

Imagine having a local chapter of students plan their own local contest. Student leaders could direct the members' review of national guidelines for their contest. They could then devise their own contest segments. For each segment, the students could create several contest options. These options could be placed into the mix of possibilities for the actual contest. The contest coordinator (usually the teacher-advisor) could select from these options to create the actual contest. Students could use these options to plan review contests before the date of the actual local contest. Imagine having students (instead of the teacher) plan a review of information that is being taught. This opens up the possibility of increased motivation.

In any local contest, judges will be needed. The local chapter could also contact business and industry persons to request their assistance in judging. This type of interaction with the real world of the workplace can help to place curriculum in context. It can also increase the public relations efforts of the program. Interaction with business and industry professionals can also raise the perceptions of importance of the skills being taught. Students would also need to follow up this process by sending thank-you letters to the judges afterward. This presents an additional opportunity for integration and opens up the possibility of partnering with an academic teacher.

Students could also be involved in planning for the types of recognition that they want to provide for participants in their local competition. By involving students in this decision, the teacher-advisor may be able to discover additional and often more meaningful items for recognition. Raising monies to fund recognition items could also be part of the local chapter's plan of work. Student inclusion in the process can be used to foster their involvement and understanding as well as their excitement and motivation. Using strategic planning, where specific tactics are planned before, during, and after a teaching lesson, can raise the quality of teaching (Marzano, Pickering, and Pollock, pg. 155). Using this type of student involvement and teacher planning to conduct a review activity: *priceless*.

Chapter Nine

Importance of the Advisor

"Setting an example is not the main means of influencing others,
it is the only means."

Albert Einstein

Impact of Teachers

Students can and should see evidence of their related CTSO throughout their school. Trophies, posters, medals, clothing items, bulletin boards, banners, etc. may be on display. This type of exposure can be important, but it is not the most important element of a CTSO. The most important element of a CTSO is their teacher-advisor. Good teachers make good advisors! Becoming a good advisor can help teachers to become better teachers.

CTSOs provide excellent materials for the teacher-advisor to use. The quality and availability of these materials should provide encouragement to any new advisor. These materials should also encourage existing advisors who are considering expanding the positive role of a CTSO in their CTE program. Curriculum materials are great, and at one time the strength of curriculum materials was thought to be the most important component of strong educational programs. Currently, enough evidence exists to prove that quality teachers provide the greatest impact on student achievement (Cummings, pg. 1-2).

Students' First View

The teacher-advisor is the face of the organization to the student. He or she represents the organization to the student. This advisor can become the person who knows all of the potential benefits of the student's CTSO participation. The level of support that this advisor provides to his or her students determines the benefits that the student will be able to gain. Whether the advisor is a new teacher or an experienced teacher who has limited his or her exposure to the organization, the advisor should gradually learn the potential student benefits. The teacher-advisor purveys the potential benefits of the CTSO to the student membership. He or she can choose to expand or limit the benefits to their students.

At the high school and post-secondary levels of education, teachers don't always get the positive feedback from their students that elementary teachers often receive. If the students of these upper-level teachers have positive thoughts about their teachers, they are more inclined to keep their positive thoughts to themselves. However, if the students of these upper-level teachers have negative thoughts about anything, they are more likely to express these opinions to their teacher. This doesn't mean that teachers don't have a positive impact or generate positive thoughts; it just means that they probably won't get a lot of positive feedback.

CTSO students tend to view their advisors in a positive light. A survey was taken of CTSO students attending the 2004 SkillsUSA National Skills and Leadership Conference in Kansas City, Missouri. When responding to the question "Please name one job or occupation that you believe can change the world" on the first annual SkillsUSA conference student survey, the top job or occupation selected was: *teacher*.

Getting Started

At first exploration of the potential student benefits, advisors may find that certain activities of their related CTSO mesh well with their existing curriculum and the advisor's personal style. These activities should become the initial source of CTSO interaction with their education program. It will take time and work to integrate these activities into the curriculum. Once fully integrated, the teacher-advisor should find that these activities are not difficult to operate. At this time, the advisor may also discover that the teacher-benefits outweigh the teacher-work needed to support these activities. Anything that motivates their students and encourages them to become better students will ultimately make the teacher's work experience more effective, more pleasant, and more rewarding.

Once teacher-advisors have completely implemented their first CTSO activities into their curriculum, they could be satisfied with efforts and stop adding activities to their education program. A good teacher is a very busy teacher, and time is limited. The features of the job usually include a constant onslaught of newly-mandated initiatives that teachers must implement. This can pressure teachers not to engage in other activities that may not be on the most recent list of new and improved mandates.

Picking up Speed

In spite of these external pressures, good teachers who want to remain good teachers should know that they must be constantly learning and evolving. This process decelerates as good teachers gain knowledge and experience, but it should never stop completely. At some stage in this learning evolution process, good teachers should take a second look at CTSO activities that were not used at first. These teacher-advisors may find that they have gained the time and/or insight to utilize the benefits of other CTSO activities. They may also find that some previously overlooked CTSO activities provide a source of knowledge that will be beneficial. The activities of these organizations can be used as tools to upgrade their educational program. As always, teacher-advisors should not try to do everything at once, but they should continue to gradually incorporate any activities that can benefit their students and program. Good teachers should not be overwhelmed, but they should not deprive themselves and their students of any of the tools of success.

Locating Tools

Where can teacher-advisors find these tools? CTSOs have many publications. Initially, new teachers may wish to find experienced teachers to explain the tools that they use to interact with the CTSO. This can lead to a good initial exposure to the goals and activities of the organization. Once exposed, teachers should realize that this information, while useful, is second-hand information. Armed with this knowledge, they may be ready to take the second step: get the information directly from the organization. Most, if not all, CTSOs publish official manuals or handbooks that describe the history, purposes, ceremonies, organizational structure, and/or activities of the CTSO. Some organizations publish information on their competitive activities. Some also have special publications that provide information specifically for advisors and/or local chapters of their national organizations. Some CTSOs have brochures describing their organization and its activities. Most of this information is usually found on their website. All CTSOs have websites:

www.bpa.org   Business Professionals of America

www.deca.org   DECA, An Association of Marketing Students

www.fcclainc.org   Family, Career, and Community Leaders of America

                     (FCCLA)

www.ffa.org   Future Farmers of America (FFA)

www.fbla/pbl.org   Future Business Leaders of America (FBLA)

www.hosa.org   Health Occupations Students of America (HOSA)

www.skillsusa.org   SkillsUSA

www.tsaweb.org   Technology Student Association (TSA)

Sparking Interest

In addition to providing knowledge and structure, teacher-advisors provide the spark to get students interested. The advisor's zeal for the potential benefits of the organization transfers to their students. It is important for the advisor to have knowledge of the organization, but he or she also needs to have high levels of enthusiasm. If the students are to be motivated by the CTSO, their teacher-advisor needs to be motivated by the CTSO. A motivated teacher-advisor is needed to lead the students into this adventure.

A beginning teacher-advisor may not start out with enough motivational experiences. He or she should feel free to borrow the experiences of veteran advisors. The veterans should have some moving stories to tell about the benefits derived by previous students. Once a new advisor has participated, he or she should start to accumulate their own success stories.

The advisor needs to motivate students in many ways. Students need to be motivated to "sign-up" to participate. After "signing-up", they need to be encouraged to "hang in there" as they prepare and practice. As the date of the activity draws near, they need their advisor to boost their confidence so that they will be ready to give their best effort to the task at hand. After the activity has ended, they may be discouraged that the outcome of their performance was less than desirable; although this may not mean that their performance was not good. In this case, the advisor needs to let them know that they performed well. If the outcome of the student's performance did not meet their expectation, the student needs to be cheered for his or her performance. They may need to be reminded of other benefits than winning an election or a medal. The advisor needs to make sure that all students derive a benefit from their participation. Advisor praise should not be in short supply.

After-Graduation Value

A Career and Technical Student Organization may be one of the first professional organizations where students have membership. The professionalism aspect should be stressed by the advisor. Students and teacher-advisors represent more than just themselves in this organization. They also represent their program, their school, and their district to the community that interacts with the CTSO. They also follow the proud traditions of their predecessors; for students, that means former students who are now members of the business community.

The professionalism of the students can be very impressive to the business and community persons that interact with CTSO activities. Students who are dressed appropriately, who act politely, and who demonstrate a professional demeanor during these interactions can make a positive impression on judges, guests, organizers, and observers. Students who aren't properly advised, guided, and taught to make this positive impression will still make an impression, but this impression might not be good for the program, school, and/or district reputation.

Advisors can inform students of the positive effect that graduates have received by citing CTSO participation during a job application process. They can teach students that this type of extra-curricular activity impresses employers in general. They can let students know that many employers in the businesses related to their CTSO also know about the students' specific CTSO and have a favorable impression of CTSO students. This impression is based upon the outstanding attitude and conduct of former students. Advisors should inspire students to continue the tradition of impressing businesspersons by demonstrating that their professional demeanor at CTSO activities is as high as the student members who preceded them. Teachers can advise these students that future student members will benefit from their proper conduct as well. Students need to know that they currently represent the quality of their CTSO as well as the quality of their career and technical education program.

Inspiration and Perspective

Teacher-advisors need to be inspired themselves. They are role models for their students. Advisors need to do more than believe in what they are inspiring students to attempt; advisors need to demonstrate these high ideals as well. Advisors need to remember that the teacher-advisors also represent their CTSO, district, school, and education program. These advisors need to model the highest level of professionalism in appropriate dress, attitude, and conduct. Advisors should keep in mind that their actions will have an impact on the future of their students. If advisors are good role models for their students, they will have a positive impact. If advisors are not good role models for their students, they will have a negative impact.

Teacher-advisors need to prepare for CTSO activities as well. They need to bring the proper attitude and the proper perspective to the contest. They need to remind themselves of their importance in this process. Advisors are the face of the CTSO to the students and to the community. It is imperative that they are prepared to have the proper look on their face at all activities.

Would teacher-advisors ever act unprofessionally in connection with a CTSO activity? Some situations arise in these activities that can put the human reaction in conflict with the professional reaction. It is often difficult to suppress the human reaction sufficiently for the professional reaction to function properly. At these times, the leadership qualities of the teacher-advisor are put to the test. If the human reaction prevails in these stressful situations, the students are the ones who suffer the consequences. Teachers must always remember that they are student role models and that they can't help children or young adults if the teachers themselves can't act like adults.

Stressful situations can happen, especially with a competitive activity. Advisors should know that all students can't win, that students should take pride in their best efforts, and that students shouldn't have to win to have a positive experience. Advisors should also know that contests can't be perfect, that you can't rerun an imperfect contest without other imperfections showing up, that you shouldn't question the judgment of the judges, and that you have to wait until next year to improve an imperfect contest. But advisors have worked hard to prepare their students for this contest, and they may also feel that this year they have a student who should win a medal. If a perceived contest imperfection "robs" their student of a medal, advisors may be tempted to have a very human, but very unprofessional reaction. They may mix their own disappointment with an obligation to stick up for their students, but this mixture could cause an explosive reaction. Or they may initially be cool and calm; but if not careful, the emotions of the students may act as a catalyst to volatility.

It is very easy for teacher-advisors to have the structure of their planned professional demeanor wrecked by the emotional reactions of their students. Students are put under a great deal of stress in competitive activities where the purpose of the activity is to differentiate scores rather than to allow students to comfortably perform their best work. The stress of competition and being judged in this situation can cause newly-learned professional habits to break down. Students can lash out at the contest design as well as imperfections in that design. Imperfections can be real or perceived. The degree of reality doesn't matter to the emotions of the student. The more that the teacher cares for his or her students, the harder it becomes for the teacher-advisor to resist the transference of these emotions. The teacher should also know that the students' negative reaction may represent their anticipation of their teacher's disappointment in their performance. If both the teacher and the students express negative reactions, the reactions can feed off of each other and escalate into a feeding frenzy.

The importance of the advisor's leadership can be seen in these situations. Good teacher-advisors have helped the students prepare their skills and their appropriate conduct for the contest, but they should also have worked before the contest to prepare the students to have realistic expectations. The expectation should be that getting a medal is not the most important thing, and students can be winners by demonstrating all of their professional skills. Good teacher-advisors will work to maintain reasonable expectations after the contest as well. They should inform students that any perceived or real problems don't affect the pride that the advisor has for the skills and effort that the students displayed. Praise and pride need to be transferred to the students after the contest. If the students have impressed the judges and observers, then that is the important message that needs to be brought to the forefront of all discussions.

If the advisor sees problems that could be corrected before the next competitive activity, the advisor needs to respond appropriately. That means politely, professionally (not emotionally), and in the appropriate setting. The appropriate setting is never in front of the students. Advisors are the role model for reaction to what happens to students in contests. The students should not even know if the advisor wishes to suggest changes, because that could lead to more questioning of contest results by the students. In many cases, it is best for advisors to wait until a few days or weeks after a contest to offer suggestions. This way, advisors can carefully prepare and prioritize their comments. Advisors can also use this time to insure that their response is professional, not emotional. Advisors need to make helpful, not critical, suggestions. Advisors who have coordinated local contests can quickly learn that criticized judges often result in constantly training replacements. Contest quality rises as good judges gain experience, but the experience level (and consequently the quality level) can't rise if a completely new crop of judges must be trained each year. It is also not a great idea to upset too many representatives of the career-related community by criticizing their performance as judges.

Accentuating Proper Positives

Advisors are the most important face of the CTSO to their students and the business community. Teacher-advisors also represent the CTSO to their bosses, the school administrators, as well. These advisors should understand that it is unfair for their students or their program to be judged by how many medals they bring back to the school. In some cases, the advisors may need to inform their supervisors that teachers should not be judged by how many medals they didn't bring back to the school. In all cases, teacher-advisors need to inform their students that they have performed in a positive manner, regardless of the contest outcome. The teacher's response will be a key component of their students' reactions.

Advisors should stress the positive consequences of the participation of all students to their supervisors. If one or more of an advisor's students do win medals at a CTSO competitive activity, the advisor needs to talk about the successes of the other students as well. Teacher-advisors should be careful how they distribute and accept praise when their students win medals. They don't want to contribute to judgments made solely on that basis. This type of judgment is not only inaccurate; it could also be used against them in the future. It is easy for a teacher to tell a supervisor that his or her career and technical program did well this year because one of the students won a medal, but would it mean that the program is doing badly in a future year if none of the students win a medal? Probably not, but teachers should keep this in mind when they report the successes of their students every year. A good teacher will be proud when one or more of the students win a medal, but this same teacher will also be proud of the performance of all students. It is important that teachers report that all of the students kept up with the students at the contests who represented the best of that state, region, district, etc. That success can be consistently reported every year.

There may be times when all or most of the students do not do well in a competition. This may happen because the contest is new to the teacher and/or the students. It may happen if a contest that they have attended many times is drastically changed. It may happen for other reasons. When this happens, good teacher-advisors don't blame the students. If the fault lies with the curriculum or the teacher, the teacher should take responsibility. If not, the teacher should share the responsibility. If it is a learning experience, the teacher should make the students understand that they have not failed and that this experience will be used to make the program stronger. When students are lost in a competition, they can often be praised for the way that they continued to try. They can be praised for their conduct in such a tense situation. They may be disappointed, but a good teacher-advisor will make every effort to make the event a positive learning experience.

The teacher-advisor needs to help the students keep the proper perspective for viewing contests. With proper encouragement, every experience can be a learning experience. Some students will be able to return to try the contest again next year. Some students will have to view the experience as preparation for the stresses of the workplace. It is the responsibility of the advisor to put the proper spin on the student experience. If the advisor is proactive and frames the upcoming contest experience in terms of courage and persistence, students will be more understanding that stepping out of their comfort level to expand their experiences is a huge part of personal growth that will take them far in their work life.

Advisor's Role

The role of the teacher-advisor is extremely important. This role should not be taken lightly, but good teachers should actively take on this role. Without an active advisor, students would not understand the potential benefits that the CTSO has to offer them. Without a professional advisor, students would not have the benefit of a good role model. The advisor can also represent the best of the organization to the community as well. The function of the advisor is so vital to the CTSO that every aspect of the job must be carefully considered and cautiously carried out. The rewards of being a good advisor are similar to the rewards of being a good teacher: helping and preparing students. Becoming a better advisor can help teachers to become better teachers. Teachers are role models for students, and better teachers will be better role models for students. This can go a long way toward changing their world.

There are many tools available to assist the advisor in this role. All of the CTSOs listed have well-organized multi-purpose materials available from their national offices. All of these CTSOs have outstanding leadership that works with their national staff to facilitate the advisor's function. State leadership and guidance is also available. The primary purpose of these resources is to promote the organization for advisors and their students.

The advisor still plays the central role for the students. The effectiveness of this co-curricular experience is greatly dependent on the local chapter advisor (NCCVSO, pg. 12). Because CTSO activities are co-curricular, every good CTE teacher should be an advisor for CTSO students. Each year, CTSOs honor some of their outstanding advisors at CTSO state and national conferences in recognition of the extreme value of good advisors. When students talk about a good advisor, they usually note the huge impact that this person has had on their life. When former students talk about a good advisor, they often cite the impact that this person has had on their success. Even the person who years later became the Executive Director for SkillsUSA cited his advisor when talking about the foundation of his success (See Preface). For CTSOs, there is no more important role than advisor.

Chapter Ten

Classroom Management

"Education is simply the soul of a society as it passes
from one generation to another."

G.K. Chesterton

Possibilities of Motivation

Education should be more than the segmented passing of tidbits of knowledge to students. It should involve stirring the possibilities of the future into a confluence of exciting concepts and ideas. The techniques of technical careers are no more important than the pride and drive that the best practitioners bring to work every day. The technical knowledge of top employees is no more vital to their occupational success than the soft skills (critical thinking, employability traits, and communication skills) that make them professional. If career and technical students are to be prepared for job success, they will need to be driven to learn at least the foundational basics of the technical competencies that comprise their career pathway. They will also need to practice the employability skills that they will need for career success, while they are learning other skills. Motivated and purposeful students help to generate a positive learning environment that is more easily managed.

CTSOs offer opportunities for increasing student motivation. They provide a chance for students to compete, or get into the game, while still in school. They offer the possibility of working as a team in competitions. CTSO activities can be used to bring business, industry, and community leaders in contact with students. In addition, students can become more involved in their education and practice some elements of self-governance through running local chapter activities. CTSOs can also be a venue for student recognition through elected office, participation, and achievement. Motivated students bring elements of self-management to their classrooms and laboratories.

Importance of Management

How important is classroom management? A lack of classroom management will quickly burn out the most energetic teacher. Constant disruptions to the teaching process will require some reaction, even though the teacher has little or no classroom management skills. Teachers will be forced either to ignore or to cope with students who are not focusing on what is being taught. Attempting to create some semblance of order from constant disorder can be an exhausting and unrewarding process for teachers.

An unmanaged classroom can disrupt the learning process for students too. Many students will stop trying to focus on the material that needs to be learned. Students who are trying to learn will become distracted by the constant disruptions caused by out of control students and the subsequent

Dale R. Derrickson, Ed.D.

interruptions that result as the teacher tries to regain control. Other students, if they are more ambivalent about learning, may decide that it is too confusing to try to learn anything and much easier to enjoy the entertainment value of chaos.

An overly managed classroom can also result in an atmosphere that is not conducive to learning. These classrooms can be too strict. In such a rigid atmosphere, students may not feel safe enough to risk failure. Failure must be risked in order for anything to be tried to its fullest. In a fearful atmosphere, cautious students may hesitate to try any new activity. When pushed to try, students may exert minimal effort. If they fail to understand, they may withdraw from asking questions. The outward appearance of some overly managed classrooms may appear neat and orderly. A closer examination may reveal students that feel uncomfortably controlled, rather than invited to learn by their teacher.

Negative Discipline

Even a seemingly innocuous event like a high school program orientation can forecast cloudy student/teacher relationships when well meaning but overbearing teachers use this stage to inform students of the rules and warn them of consequences of breaking the rules. It is incongruous that this is more likely to happen at a high school than at an elementary school (Sullo, pg. 96-97). Any positive effects on behavior that punishment might have on younger children are less pronounced in older children (Kagan and Segal, pg. 174). Too often our tradition of schooling has focused on student failures and limitations rather than building on student successes and possibilities (Bonstingl, pg. 39). High school teachers may easily fall into the trap of thinking that their power over students lies in rules and consequences. Although rules and consequences may need to be communicated, teachers need to accentuate the positive to inspire students to follow the guidelines of a program in a state of engagement.

Educators can't forget that CTSOs are involved in preparing CTE students for the workplace. While companies have rules and procedures that must be followed, they also have consequences for not following those rules. Any infraction becomes part of the employee's record. Serious infractions usually result in immediate dismissal. CTE programs can't send students into the workplace who are used to interacting with authority figures by habitually breaking the rules and getting punished. CTE teachers can't make recommendations to employers like, "If you threaten this student every day, this student will perform at his or her highest skill level for you." Employers offering high-skill, high-wage jobs won't long tolerate much negative behavior from their employees. They expect a lot of self-actuated professional behavior for their companies and ultimately, their customers.

CTE students should be learning and practicing the skills that they will need on the job while they are in school. These skills include technical skills and employability skills. Teachers who use negative reinforcement constantly set up an adversarial relationship between themselves and their students. The CTE learning environment should become a simulated workplace for students. In this simulation, the teacher takes the role of the supervisor and the student plays the role of employee. The first rule for getting along with your supervisor is to realize that the boss is not the enemy (Rigolosi, pg. 20).

Elements of Success

There are many elements to successful classroom management. Some of these elements are <u>reactive</u>, where the teacher properly reacts to different situations to quell or prevent a disruption to classroom activities. Other elements are <u>proactive</u>, where the teacher acts to prevent the occurrence of disruptive situations. Both out-of-control and overly-controlled classrooms result from insufficient positive proactive efforts. Career and Technical Student Organization activities can be part of proactive classroom management. This type of management leads to more student self-control.

When examining any type of classroom management model, the preferred style of the individual teacher cannot be ignored. Individual teachers have their own personal style of human interaction. Each teacher should also develop his or her own personal, but effective, style of teaching. Every teacher (who wants to become successful) will also acquire their own personal style of classroom management. As teachers observe other teachers and study classroom management systems, they need to find the elements of these systems with which they feel they can become comfortable. If a classroom management system or style doesn't fit a teacher's personality and beliefs, it would be extremely difficult for that system or style to enable good classroom management for that teacher.

No matter what style the teacher adopts, some facts are universally evident. Unmotivated students easily become bored. Boredom can lead to disruptive behaviors, as students look for something other than participating in the program to occupy their time. Keeping students motivated and actively engaged will prevent many of these problems. It should be remembered that the only activities teachers should have to offer students are their program activities. Teachers work hard to make these activities as interesting and exciting as possible, but students who don't actively participate will be very bored.

Workplace Relativity

Career and technical education already has the potential to offer many things that can motivate students. The hands-on activities of the career and technical laboratory are often different from the activities that dominate many academic classroom settings. This concrete illustration of ideas can cater to the learning styles of students who haven't been very successful in more abstract settings. It can also provide additional insight for students who have been successful in more abstract settings.

Career and technical programs should illustrate a connection with business and industry. Students often question why they need to learn certain subject matter and can effectively tune out educational efforts when they think subjects are not important. Good programs are designed to have a direct link with high skill, high wage jobs. Activities that strengthen this link and define this link for students can help provide the answer to "Why do I need to know this?"

Successful companies in the modern workplace work under a different structure than the old factory style of management. In that old, top-down style of management, employees performed repetitious jobs that required little thought once the basics were learned. Orders came from top management (through middle management) down to the workers. This vertical style of management was effective when the workplace was not as fast-paced and technically-complicated as it is today. Due to the complex technology involved in the modern workplace, decisions must be dispersed both vertically and horizontally. This requires a shared approach to management in order to achieve success

(Carnevale, Gainer, and Meltzer, pg. 379). In many cases, shared management requires workers to be self-managed.

Teacher-advisors need to remember that they are attempting to pass on the soul of their career to their students. This reaches beyond simply passing down the technical skills of the career area. While technical skills are important, personal skills may be even more important. Students need to develop enthusiasm about their career area and pride in this area to become successful in the workplace (Carnevale, Gainer, and Meltzer, pg. 234). They also need to practice the employability skills needed to thrive in their professional careers.

Students need to see the connection between the classroom/laboratory and the workplace. The types of student behaviors that are acceptable in both of these arenas need to be learned and practiced in the high school setting. Teachers need to teach students the importance of acquiring these skills for workplace success and to relate their practice to classroom/laboratory activities. Once this connection is made, the transformation of the classroom/laboratory into a simulated workplace should help to provide students with essential soft skills and, at the same time, assist with classroom management.

Inspiration Lowers Perspiration

One of the things that distinguishes teachers who inspire their students from teachers who do not inspire their students is that the former group is initially more concerned that a positive learning environment is being created and less concerned (initially) with academic results (Sullo, pg.102). Given the importance of fostering an environment where students learn and practice their soft skills along with the importance of facilitating the learning of motivated students in an environment where they feel safe to act on their motivation, this should be a consideration for CTE teachers. If CTE teachers are successful in creating this inspirational atmosphere, both employability skills and technical skills will be able to develop easily.

Inspired students are motivated to perform. Instructing these students and guiding them through their performances requires less teacher perspiration than attempting to push uninspired students to learn and to perform. CTE teachers should already know the exciting possibilities of the career area that they teach. CTSO activities can complement the CTE program's efforts to convey these possibilities to high school students. The interaction of business, industry, and the community with students through CTSO activities provides a lens through which students can more clearly see the future importance of their career area. The respect that this external constituency demonstrates through their program support can generate additional excitement among the students. An awareness of the skills needed for success in upcoming competitions can motivate students to delve deeper into the curriculum as they strive to receive the recognition that should accompany competition. The purposes and ideals of these organizations can influence student motivation in a positive manner.

As students increase their motivation, they become more self-actualized. CTSOs often offer publications that celebrate models of student achievement. CTSOs provide another venue for self-management: the local chapter. CTSOs also provide detailed guidelines for members of the local chapter and for planning the activities of the local chapter. To the extent practicable, the local chapter should be operated by the students. This provides an arena for CTE students to learn and practice their management skills. If students are able to plan their program of work to use their career skills to serve their community, they will truly be able to share fruits of their labor through community service activities. This can provide a great deal of another motivator: self-satisfaction.

As students take greater responsibility for their education, the teacher becomes more of a coach than a lecturer. In the atmosphere created by this, the students find their education more satisfying and more fun. The teacher can also find his or her role more satisfying and more fun. Grades are not the only motivator for student success. Incorporating CTSO motivators into the CTE program can lead to more student success. This is one of the purposes of CTSOs. The employability and self-management skills that students can bring to their careers create the possibility of high levels of success.

Safe Learning Environment

Creating an atmosphere of safety for students in the CTE classroom and laboratory requires more than just classroom management that is controlling enough to properly supervise safety rules and procedures. It is important to create an atmosphere of safety and security, where students do not fear making the type of mistakes that accompany an active learning process. Some of the best learning experiences and many important scientific discoveries have risen out of mistakes. Students should be encouraged to fully participate in classroom/laboratory activities. They need to know that their teacher recognizes that mistakes are part of the learning process. They should feel confident that their attempts will not be overly criticized if they make a mistake. The natural human learning process is learning by doing; this often means also learning from our mistakes. An effective classroom and laboratory atmosphere should invite students to learn without fear of being less than perfect.

How students feel about their chances for success in a teacher's class can determine the amount of effort they put into learning in that class (Cummings, pg. 132). At the early stages of the learning process, effort is more important than outcome. If formative assessments are used, their less than perfect outcomes can provide information that can help teachers to work with student efforts to build better understanding. This is predicated upon a learning environment where the teacher praises the formative efforts of students. CTSO activities can sometimes be used as formative assessments by the effective teacher-advisor. They can be highly effective if used properly. Sometimes this helps if the teacher views these tests as being a test of their efforts as much as a test of the students' efforts.

When CTSO activities take the form of a chapter election or a local contest, they are often viewed in a more high-stakes light by students. This does not mean that these activities are being used for grading, but that students are more likely not to view these as "second-chance" events (at least in the relatively near future). The perceived finality of chapter elections and local contests can make students feel that their success is being measured. To make these events positive experiences for all requires the proactive teacher to define their realistic expectations for the students before these events transpire. After the event, the properly focused advisor will praise the efforts of the students. The properly focused teacher will also lavishly praise the elements of the efforts that had positive outcomes before pointing out any errors.

When students move to a regional, state, or national CTSO activity, they may view the stakes as even higher. If not properly prepared, they may view not participating as winning. Teacher-advisors need to coach these students ahead of the event to help the students understand the value of giving their best effort. If not properly coached beforehand, they may feel that they let their teacher, their school, or their state down. Regardless of the outcome, their achievement needs to be celebrated.

If properly used, CTSO activities can be an asset for classroom activities. Their potential for motivation, review, leadership, and learning is great. Still, the events of these organizations contain a lot of competitive activities. One of the strengths of good CTE programs is their ability to take students who were previously less than fully successful and provide these students with many opportunities to achieve success. Teacher-advisors need to be careful that CTSO activities do not become a way for students to lose. It takes a lot of preparation and positive reinforcement to make certain that <u>all</u> participants come out feeling like winners. To do anything less would be to remove the students' safety net. This would create an unsafe and overly managed learning environment.

Whose Classroom Is It?

Many times dedicated CTE teachers immerse themselves so fully in their program that they tend to personalize their classroom. It is not uncommon when they approach administrators, advisory members, etc. for them to initiate their requests by stating "I need". While this dedication is admirable, it is much more effective to launch these statements with the phrase "The students need". If the first type of lead-in is used, others may get the false impression that the request is only something that the teacher needs.

Teachers tend to take possession of their classroom in other ways as well. "My classroom, my rules" is not an unusual sentiment. CTE teachers often use their classrooms and laboratories to simulate workplaces in order to foster student practice of appropriate workplace behaviors. In simulated workplaces, the teacher represents "the boss" where the supervisor's rules also represent the company rules and procedures.

CTE teachers need to remember that their course is not always a graduation requirement, like many academic courses. If students do need a CTE class for graduation credits, they do not always need the teacher's specific course for graduation; often, they could take another class or transfer to a different program. Like a store owner who has propriety over their store, CTE teachers have customers that need to be invited to enter and stay in order for them to stay in business. These customers are their students. Furthermore, for this business to prosper, their "customers" need to buy-in by actively participating in the activities.

Barbara Blackburn points out that students need to have classroom ownership in order to be fully committed to the educational process. She cites three steps to encourage active involvement:

1. Choice

2. Voice

3. Leadership

Blackburn describes the <u>Choice</u> step as the starting point where teachers allow students to make some decisions within the confines of limited choices that are initially made available to the students. <u>Voice</u> is the next step, where the teacher allows students to help to determine or add to the choices. This is a more shared approach to decision-making. Finally, the <u>Leadership</u> step provides students with defined roles for regular participation in deciding issues (Blackburn, pg. 103-106).

Allowing student participation does not mean that the teacher gives up his or her control completely. Teachers must set the parameters for this process, and they still decide which issues will be open for student direction and which issues will remain under the teacher's control. How much control is given over to the students should depend on the teacher's individual style. It also should be contingent upon how much experience a teacher has with this process. Teachers who have less experience with this process should start slowly, learn as they go, and increase student control only as they feel comfortable. Students must also gain experience in this process as it moves forward.

Operating a local CTSO chapter offers student opportunities for leadership and voice. Control may start with the planning and operation of CTSO activities. In the beginning, inexperienced advisors may limit the choices available to students. As they gain experience with this process, advisors may feel more comfortable with expanding the students' options. As teacher-advisors see the increased motivation that classroom and CTSO ownership can create, they will be more inclined to expand the students' options.

Students will typically push the option envelope. Some control gives them some ownership. Ownership stimulates motivation which, in turn, encourages students to do more. Some of the students' requests for more ownership and control will be logical steps in either the students' or teacher's learning process with this concept. The teacher-advisor may be ready for some of the student requests and totally surprised by others. The teacher-advisor should keep in mind that explaining to students why they can't have control over some aspect of a CTSO or classroom activity does not need to bring this process to an abrupt halt; it can serve to refocus the students on activities that they can influence.

If the teacher-advisor is totally surprised by a student ownership/control request, he or she can postpone a decision by telling the students that the proposal will require some thought. After careful consideration, the request can be accepted or denied. Any denials should be accompanied by a reasonable explanation. If the teacher-advisor can't come up with a reasonable explanation for denying a request, perhaps more thought and a possible consideration of acceptance is needed. Of course students, like employees in a workplace, can't have full ownership and control. The modern workplace, however, is encouraging the ownership and increasing the control of their employees.

Teachers should give the students some ownership of the classroom/laboratory. They should let the students get involved in the decision-making process. Teacher-advisors should let students have a better understanding of upcoming activities through planning the activities. When the students get involved, they will also do some of the work. The students will start to participate in their own motivation. Teachers should let customers (the students) give them some feedback; it may help in refining activities to make them more palatable to students.

Teachers should use this process to get students to more actively participate in their education. It is rewarding to watch them become leaders. When this happens, teachers can push students less and teach the students more. It is a nice experience when their often exhausting job becomes easier and more satisfying. Once teachers try it, they will get better at it. Once they get good at it, they will never go back! Teacher-advisors should use their CTSO local chapter as a tool to help make this happen. The purpose of CTSOs can offer exciting possibilities for teachers as well as for their students!

Chapter Eleven

Business, Industry, and Community Participation

"The future is being purchased by the present."

Samuel Johnson

CTE Connections

New CTE courses must be designed to reflect the knowledge, understandings, and skills needed for a career area (Bottoms, Pucel, and Phillips, pg. 31). Curriculum designers who do not collaborate with businesses and their community would be making a serious mistake (Finch and Crunkilton, pg. 88-89). Key business, industry, and community members should be part of the constituency that aids, advises, and participates in all aspects of the CTE program (Finch and McGough, pg. 160-161). If effective labor organizations exist for a specific career program, their leaders can be a valuable resource of community members.

CTE programs must constantly interact with business, industry, and their community. This interaction is needed to create new programs and to modify existing programs so that students are educated in the full spectrum of employment needs for business and industry in their community. If the abilities of students are more closely matched to the employment needs in their community, their chances of career entry and success are much higher.

In 2007, a national poll of leaders of U.S. business coalitions was undertaken by Dehavilland Associates. The types of organizations targeted included business roundtables, chambers of commerce, trade associations, workforce development groups, manufacturers' councils, and economic development groups. The leaders of these business groups ranked workforce preparedness as their top educational priority. They also reported that they spend more than twice as much of their precious time working at the high school level than they spent working at the elementary, middle-school, or post-secondary level (DHA, pg. 1-4).

Given the extra materials and equipment needed to operate most CTE programs, support from business, industry, and community leaders is also needed. The expertise of these leaders is also a valuable commodity that can assist in supporting CTE programs. Whether this support takes the form of additional tax dollars or direct donations of time, money, or equipment, this external constituency of leaders can help provide the resources to create and operate a successful CTE program. Good CTE programs cannot become great CTE programs without a high level of interaction with these leaders (DeHavilland, pg.1-4).

Student Workplace Connections

High school students who complete a CTE pathway have the opportunity to experience benefits in the workplace after graduation. To take advantage of these benefits, they also have to find a job in a field related to the CTE program that they completed. If high school CTE graduates are able to do this, they can earn high wages and experience low unemployment as they pursue their careers. Unfortunately, less than half of CTE students are placed in related jobs (Gray and Herr, pg. 261).

Even in the best high school CTE programs, some students will change their career goals. The best programs will, however, provide connections to the workplace for their students. These programs will maintain close contacts with business, labor, industry, and community leaders. These contacts can result in curriculum, equipment, tools, and cooperative employment opportunities that are closely aligned to their labor market segment and the needs of employers in that segment.

The School-to-Work Opportunities Act became federal law in 1994. It provided seed money to create and strengthen ties between education and employers. One of the key strategies emphasized by this act was to foster collaboration between these two groups. While the funding provided by this act has run its course, the ideals supported by the act are still relevant.

Teachers who are not willing to make and maintain connections with employers are short-changing their students' futures. If a program has no connections, the teacher should start to create them. If the program has connections, the teacher might consider strengthening them. Strong connections result in stalwart programs. Increasing connections can produce more student opportunities. Teacher-advisors can use CTSO activities to strengthen these connections. They can't shrink from this responsibility when their students' futures are at stake. The best high school CTE programs should strive to beat the national average of less than half of students connecting in program related jobs.

Possible Concern

This vital <u>external constituency</u> may already exist at the CTE level without being a part of the program's CTSO activities. The same leaders that participate in cooperative employment and/or advisory committees for the local program can be a resource for locating participants in CTSO activities. In some cases, teacher-advisors may hesitate to tap this resource for further activities. These advisors may have concerns that discourage them from fully taking advantage of these contacts.

How many times can teacher-advisors ask the same leaders to participate in yet another activity? These important people usually have very busy schedules. Can we ask them to do more? If we ask them to participate in more activities, will they run out of time? Will they stop doing one important activity if asked to participate in another important activity? Will members of this external constituency who try to take part in every activity get "burned out" and completely stop participating in everything? These are fair questions that can represent genuine concerns, but these concerns should not prevent advisors from approaching the leaders of their constituency.

Teacher-advisors should approach their cooperative education employers, advisory committee members, and any other business/community leaders by stating what assistance their CTSO might need. Advisors should let the leaders determine their own appropriate level of involvement. The high level of commitment that these leaders may have will sometimes be surprising. If a leader states that increasing efforts in one area may necessitate a decrease in other efforts, the teacher-advisor must decide which is more appropriate.

There are other options. Other options include asking these leaders if they can bring in other leaders or employees to assist with CTSO activities. These people have contacts in their companies, their industry, and their community. These contacts can be a valuable resource to CTE and CTSOs. If the leaders don't have the time or inclination to contact these people, another option is for the teacher-advisor to initiate contact if names and addresses or phone numbers can be supplied. The teacher-advisor could also contact companies, labor organizations, and industry organizations on their own as well. Teacher-advisors can also guide their students to become part of the contact effort.

Importance of Feedback

Feedback is needed to provide information that is essential to keeping the efforts of personnel on track (Goleman, pg. 150). Business, industry, and community leaders can be indispensable personnel for CTE and CTSOs, and they will need feedback to understand how vital their efforts have been to the success of CTSO activities. If this feedback is used to stress the positive aspects of the interaction of the school community and this external constituency, it can provide more than a cursory reassurance to these groups. It can also be used to express the deep gratitude that the school community has for the crucial efforts of this constituency. If correctly used, positive reinforcement can keep them coming back. Positive feedback may encourage some members of this external constituency to increase their efforts.

This feedback should include not only the success of the activity, but also the impact that this type of activity has on the motivation and (highly related to motivation) education of students. A personal thanks before, during, and/or after an activity that is not too repetitive and is also placed in the proper context is not overkill. If the activity generates a written program or pamphlet, listing these external participants is also effective. Providing small gifts to judges and other activity supporters is another idea that is often used. Some CTSOs also provide special awards or plaques for honored, long-time supporters. Providing certificates for participation can be positive; these certificates can even be more valued if they contain student signatures. A student word of thanks at an event can work wonders if it is appropriately worded and if it comes from the heart. Student thank-you letters can also be used to enhance feedback. Imagine the impact of a thank-you note signed by many students.

Good feedback to supporters and sponsors can help provide a positive answer to their question, "Why do I continue to come back every year?" While some external participants may become involved to hunt for better employees or to advertise to future customers, the best support comes from those who want to make a positive difference in the lives of students. The power of feedback to motivate individual performance is well known (Boyett and Conn, pg.77). These leaders represent an external constituency that doesn't have to come back into the schools. Effective feedback can result in higher levels of "come back". Businesses often use the term "Return on Investment". When attempting to keep these leaders coming back to support their CTE and CTSO programs, teacher-advisors can consider feedback efforts to be an "Investment in Return".

Circle of Benefits

CTE programs and CTSO chapters both need business, industry, and community participation to function at the highest level of quality. The advice and support of this external constituency is vital to fulfilling the roles of CTE and CTSOs. Because CTSOs should be an integral curricular activity of CTE programs, the duality of potential benefits is inseparable. The concern of overloading the participants has already been addressed. A view of the possibilities of the relationship of external constituents with CTE and CTSOs reveals a potential circle of benefits.

CTE administrators should encourage and assist advisors of local CTSO chapters because the chapters can bring the work world and the school into a closer working relationship (Wenrich, Wenrich, and Galloway, pg. 134). Finch and McGough proposed that these administrators arrange advisory committee meetings three to four times per year. They also placed the responsibility of creating agendas for each meeting on the administrators (Finch and McGough, pg. 164). Keeping lines of communication open between the school and its external constituency is important for program assistance and public relations. Due to the work involved in planning meetings, most advisory committees are not able to meet as many as three or four times every year. Those that do may eventually run out of fresh agenda topics.

CTSO activities provide another venue for interaction between the school and its external constituency. Informal discussions can arise during these activities. Some contests may serve as informal appraisals of student performance. The opportunity to view students demonstrating their abilities can be more exciting than committee meetings. The performance of all of the students participating in a CTSO contest can be very impressive to this external constituency. No one can build support for the students better than the students themselves.

Since the types of external participants is the same for CTE committees and CTSO activities, their combined activities offer more contact with the same types of persons or even the same persons. Increasing the number of interactions possible can also serve to assist in recruiting a larger number of participants. CTE can recruit for CTSOs, and CTSOs can recruit for CTE. The interactions and the participants in these interactions are mutually beneficial. Business and industry must be at the table to build effective CTE programs (Gordon, pg. 240). They may sit down more often and in greater numbers if CTSOs can provide another meal to attract them.

National Participation

Do you remember the Future Craftsmen of America? The primary mention of this now defunct organization in this book was to note that it ceased to exist due to lack of industry and labor support. Current national CTSOs seemed to have learned (either from this or from other lessons) the importance of the participation of business and industry, which includes professional and labor organizations. Each has garnered support for their national activities.

Tim Lawrence, Executive Director of National SkillsUSA, often states that the largest single week of corporate volunteerism takes place at SkillsUSA's National Skills and Leadership Conference (NLSC) in Kansas City, Missouri. In 2005, Tim cited the business, industry, and labor partners who supported the $25 million SkillsUSA Championships (Lawrence, pg. 5). The cost of the 2007 SkillsUSA NLSC increased to over $32 million, and corporate support rose to help meet the challenge. This certainly is an impressive example of support, but all CTSOs solicit and receive support from business and industry.

National CTSOs have business and industry partners on their corporate boards, advisory boards, and as supporting members of their student foundations. These national CTSO partners sponsor or otherwise contribute support for fund raising, contests, and other conference activities. They assist the CTSOs by providing judging, equipment, scholarships, and materials. These corporate partners buy advertising and may even sponsor national officer activities.

These corporate education partners are highly valued by national CTSOs. National CTSO offices usually have one or more persons assigned to solicit from and work with these partners. National CTSOs sometimes bring their national officers to meet with business and industry partners. These partners have the further opportunity to advertise at CTSO national functions. They are sometimes listed on national CTSO websites. Each year, national CTSOs distribute recognition awards to some of these corporate education partners. These partners contribute millions of dollars in direct contributions as well as their time and other assistance to national CTSOs. At times, some of these corporate partners have even worked with national CTSO offices to support federal CTE legislation.

State and Local Participation

State CTSO offices may not be able to employ a full-time staff member to develop relationships with corporate education partners. State offices still have these relationships, albeit on a smaller scale than their national CTSO offices. State offices will maintain contacts to provide judges for state events. State offices will also solicit scholarships and other prizes. State offices may also receive direct donations. Some of these donations may be cash donations. Other donations may be sponsorship of contest(s) or conference(s). Some of these donors may initiate their affiliation with the national office, but some of these donors may have first affiliation with the state CTSO.

Local chapters may sometimes benefit from business and industry relationships that were developed at the state or national level. Local chapters also need to reach out to local business and industry leaders in order to have judges and advisory committee members. Bringing these leaders into the program and exposing them to the guidance, judging assistance, and financial needs of the program often bears the fruit of financial assistance. This assistance may be for the CTE or the CTSO program. It may take the form of material and equipment donations. This assistance may involve donations of the valuable time of these community leaders. It may take the form of bringing in other leaders to further expand participation. Any support offered is usually beneficial.

Public Relations

CTE interaction with business, industry, and community leaders is needed to support and shape the quality of the program. Achieving quality is an ongoing process, but when quality programs exist the community needs to know about these quality programs. When quality students are leaving these programs, the community also needs to know about these quality students. There is a compelling need for public relations efforts since CTE programs need public awareness and support to continue to expand and improve (Finch and McGough, pg. 165).

The community at large needs to know that their community educational institution is producing a quality product. This community provides the local tax dollars needed to continue the institution's programs. This support should not be taken for granted. With the constant introduction of new initiatives in education, the spotlight tends to migrate toward the latest educational project.

The business community also needs to know that their needs for quality prospective employees are being met. Many educational reforms are initiated by business demands. While many CTE programs focus on specific job training, these reforms are often directed toward more overarching academic and behavior goals. These goals are aimed at producing the more generic version of a good employee. Quality CTE programs utilize CTSO activities to foster these generic traits while still focusing on a more specific career. When students approach the businesses and industries in their community, they also hope that the people they approach are aware of skills that they gained from their CTE and CTSO programs.

CTSOs should be viewed as a publicity tool for teachers (Scott and Sarkees-Wircenski, pg. 305). Teachers can showcase the technical, academic, and employability skills of their students to the community by inviting them in to act as judges. Student generated invitations and thank-you letters can be used to demonstrate student skills. Students from local chapters can demonstrate their citizenship skills by performing community service. If this community service utilizes their technical and employability skills as well, it represents another level of skill demonstration.

These student activities need to find their way into the media, when possible. Small local newspapers and radio/TV stations may be more receptive to these stories than bigger media companies; however, if the activity has a more regional, state, or national basis, the larger companies may be interested. Additional interest can be sparked by something that is new or unusual, such as students raising a large amount of money for a charity or the first all-male nursing team to enter state competition.

Other activities can be newsworthy as well. When students win elections at any level, this is news. When students win competitions, this should be published somewhere. Teachers must always get the approval of their administration for any media contact. There may be a district administrator responsible for media relations. If so, this is a person that the CTSO teacher-advisor needs to get to know. If not, the teacher-advisor needs to get the addresses of media contacts and learn how to write press releases. Sending out press releases to several sources does not mean that every source will pick up the story, but none of them will pick it up if they are not informed. Every press release must include:

1. Who (participants form the basis of human interest)

2. What (explain it as if the reader has no prior knowledge)

3. When (give the date and time; it should not be old news)

4. Where (location and the significance of the location)

5. Why (why this is important to potential readers; a human interest angle adds significance)

Public Relations Professionals

If the school district has a media relations specialist, this can be a valuable tool in many ways. This person should already have contact addresses for a press release. This person should also have experience in writing press releases. It is reasonable that this person would want the CTSO advisor (or the students) to write the initial version of the press release, and then edit it for final release. One of the most important things that a media relations specialist can have is personal contacts. Personal contacts know who this person is and expect to see press releases. Often, media personnel use these contacts to their advantage. If they are writing a story, they may contact media relations specialists to get a quote that they may need to flesh out the story. If reporters rely on a media relations specialist when they need story sources, they may feel somewhat obligated to accept a press release from that source.

If the teacher-advisor's district does not have a media relations specialist, one or more of their external constituency of community partners may have a media specialist. Large companies and community organizations often have someone with media expertise on their staff. If the advisor needs help publicizing an activity that involves community partners, these partners may be amenable to a dual publicity effort through their media expert. Keep in mind that the partners' support of CTSO activities is community service for them. Why wouldn't they want some of this community service to be known by the public? Their media specialist may even be part of their public relations department.

Assistance in creating public relations efforts or working with public relations experts can be found in CTSOs. They offer public relations information and training for advisors. They may offer sample press releases for winners of national conferences. They may offer media relations training at national and regional conferences. Some of this training and information are available on-line. CTSO websites also are valuable references for reporters looking for more story sources. Interest in local chapter activities may be stimulated by press releases from national CTSO offices. Once again, teacher-advisors looking for materials and information should be able to find that their CTSO has already created them.

Specialization and Obscurity

When it was first developed, the main focus of secondary public education was to provide academic education and serve the needs of college-bound students (Giachino and Gallington, pg. 15). The vast contributions of CTE have not caused modern society to completely overturn this view. Most state testing efforts focus on academic testing. The vast majority of young people expect to graduate from a four-year college (Gordon, pg. 220). College costs keep rising, but parents still want their students to attend college. The United States Government responded to this situation by adding Section 529 to the Internal Revenue Code to allow state-sponsored college savings plans and prepaid tuition plans that are exempt from federal taxes. The public education spotlight is not always focused on CTE and CTSOs.

CTE programs are highly specialized. This specialization may lead them to be known only by the small section of the public with whom these programs already interact. This specialization may obscure the general public's view of the good works of individual programs.

CTSOs can help to address this problem. They bring together entire general classifications of CTE programs. They function as national advocates for their focused-CTE area in a manner similar to the way that other industry organizations advertise and advocate for their professional members. By gathering together through their CTSOs, CTE programs can expand their strength. To maintain and raise the quality of their CTE, teacher-advisors cannot allow their students to endeavor in obscurity. CTE teacher-advisors must seek to broaden their base of support with business, industry, and the community. As they seek to expand the public's knowledge of their CTE program, they need to recognize that their CTSO can become a springboard for their efforts. The public knowledge base can moreover include governmental entities.

The Delaware Model

CTSOs in the State of Delaware have enjoyed financial support from their State's government for many years. In addition to providing state-level advisors through the Delaware Department of Education, the State budget includes monies to subsidize CTSO activities. This subsidy has been instrumental in helping to control the costs of state conferences and other CTSO statewide activities for Delaware CTE students. Efforts of the Delaware Career and Technical Student Organization Council have facilitated the advocacy of the Delaware Advisory Committee on Career and Technical Education (DACCTE) as DACCTE periodically requests increases in Delaware CTSO funding.

To assist in keeping this support active, each year State Officers from all of the Delaware CTSOs gather in the State Capital where they meet with the Governor and the State Legislators. An officer from every CTSO makes a speech in each house of the legislature, telling them of the value of these organizations to students and thanking them for their support. The legislature issues a Concurrent Resolution supporting the CTSOs, and the student officers present flowers that were grown by local FFA chapters to the Governor and State Legislators. Partly as a result of these ongoing efforts, Delaware CTSOs and their corresponding CTE programs enjoy a solid foundation of support from their state government.

Partners for Future

Business, industry, and community leaders are concerned about the future. This is precisely why they got involved in the movement toward high-stakes academic testing. While many in the high school community have interpreted this movement as another focus on four-year college preparation, business and industry leaders (especially those involved with specialized career training) see a broader picture. They know that academic skills will be needed for their employees to participate in the types of lifelong learning needed to keep up with future changes in their industry. They also know that seventy percent of jobs in the workplace will not require a four-year college degree (Gordon, pg. 216).

When national-level and state-level educators seek input from business, industry, and community leaders, they often ask for a generic viewpoint of what their students need. As the question is framed, the answer is often framed. Academic and employability skills are usually stressed. When high school educators pose this question to leaders as related to a specific career area, they often get this answer plus another answer. The other answer is that students will need to explore and gain skills relevant to a specific career area. At times, these leaders who are focused on a specific career area will sometimes express many of the same frustrations that teacher-advisors express regarding the movement of the spotlight away from CTE. If they are experiencing or predicting shortages of qualified employees, their frustration levels may be high.

CTE and CTSOs need to include these business, industry, and community (including labor) leaders as partners in the process. The support and input of these leaders is invaluable. These leaders often need CTE and CTSOs as badly as CTE and CTSOs need them. The concern for these leaders can be great if they realize that their future lies in CTE students. The advocacy of businesses, industry, and community can shine a light on these education efforts. CTSOs provide another avenue to bring these leaders to CTE students. Good career and technical education teachers should realize that business, industry, labor, CTE, and CTSOs must be closely linked in order for educators to provide a high quality experience for their students. These educators will view CTSOs as a vital tool for achieving the goal of high quality, well-rounded education for their students. If this tool didn't already exist, they would need to invent it. This tool has a valuable purpose, and it offers unlimited possibilities.

References

Abraham, Ansley A. and Creech, Joseph D. *Reducing Remedial Education: What Progress are States Making?* Atlanta, GA: Southern Regional Education Board, 1999.

ACTE. *CTSO Guide to Accessing Federal Perkins Funds.* Alexandria, VA: Association for Career and Technical Education, 1999.

ACTE. *Perkins Act of 2006: The Official Guide.* Alexandria, VA: Association for Career and Technical Education, 2006.

ACTE. "Reinventing the American High School: A Position Paper". Alexandria, VA: Association for Career and Technical Education, 2006.

ACTE Online. "Take Action-Online Advocacy Tool Kit-Talking Points-The Importance of CTE." Association for Career and Technical Education, 12/18/06 from www.acteonline.org/takeaction/toolkit-talking

AVA. *The AVA Guide to the Carl D. Perkins Vocational and Applied Technology Act of 1990.* Alexandria, VA: American Vocational Association, 1992.

AVA. *Making the Case for School-to-Careers and Vocational Education.* Alexandria, VA: American Vocational Association, 1997.

AVA. *The Official Guide to the Perkins Act of 1998.* Alexandria, VA: American Vocational Association, 1998.

Barlow, Melvin T. "Historical Background of Vocational Education", *Vocational Education in the 1990s: Major Issues.* Albert J. Paulter, Jr. Editor. Ann Arbor, MI: Prakken Publications, Inc., 1990.

Baum, S. and Payea, K. *Education Pays Update.* Washington, D.C.: College Board, 2005.

Baum, S.; Payea, K.; Steele, P.; McCrakin, S.; Goldman, J; and Brodigan, D. *Trends in College Pricing.* Washington, D.C.: College Board, 2005.

Blackburn, Barbara R. *Classroom Motivation from A to Z: How to Engage your Students in Learning.* Larchmont, NY: Eye on Education, Inc., 2005.

BPA. *Conducting Ceremonies.* Columbus, OH: Business Professionals of America, 2004.

Bird, Caroline. *The Case Against College.* New York, NY: David McKay Company, Inc., 1975.

Bloch, Deborah Perlmutter. *How To Get A Good Job And Keep It.* Lincolnwood, IL: VGM Career Horizons Division of NTC Publishing Group, 1993.

Bonstingl, John Jay. *Schools of Quality.* Alexandria, VA: Association for Supervision and Curriculum Development, 2nd Edition, 1996.

Boyle, James E., et.al. *The Country Life of the Nation.* Chapel Hill, NC: The University of North Carolina Press, 1930.

Bottoms, Gene; Pucel, David J.; and Phillips, Ione. *Designing Challenging Vocational Courses.* Atlanta, GA: Southern Regional Education Board, 1997.

Bottoms, Gene; Presson, Alice; and Johnson, Mary. *Making High Schools Work: Through Integration of Academic and Vocational Education.* Atlanta, GA: Southern Regional Education Board, 1992.

Boyett, Joseph H. and Conn, Henry P. *Workplace 2000: The Revolution Reshaping American Business.* New York, NY: Plume Division of Penguin Books, 1992.

Bridgeland, John M.; DiIulio, John J.,Jr.; and Morison, Karen B. "The Silent Epidemic: Perspectives of High School Dropouts," *Straight A's: Public Education Policy and Progress,* Vol. 6, No. 5, Alliance for Excellent Education, March 6, 2006

Brooks, Jacqueline G. and Brooks, Martin G. *in search of understanding: The Case for Constructivist Classrooms.* Alexandria, VA: Association for Supervision and Curriculum Development, 1999.

Brustein, Michael and Mahler, Marty. *The One Stop Guide to the Perkins Act of 1998.* Washington, DC: Brustein & Manasevit, 1998.

Camp, William G.; Jackson, Renee S.; Buser, Bryan R.; and Baldwin, Eliza T. *Vocational Student Organizations and Student Achievement.* Berkeley, CA: National Center for Research in Vocational Education, 2000.

Carnevale, Anthony P.; Gainer, Leila J.; and Meltzer, Ann S. *Workplace Basics: The Essential Skills Employers Want.* San Francisco, CA: Jossey-Bass Publishers, 1990.

Choy, Susan P. and Carroll, C. Dennis. *Debt Burden: A Comparison of 1992-93 and 1999-200 Bachelor's Degree Recipients a Year After Graduating.* Washington, D.C.: National Center for Education Statistics, 2005.

Covey, Stephen R. *The Seven Habits of Highly Effective People.* New York, NY: Fireside – Simon & Shuster, Inc., 1990.

Cummings, Carol. *Teaching Makes A Difference.* Snohomish, WA: Snohomish Publishing Company, Second Edition, 1991.

DECA. *DECA's Chapter Management System.* Reston, VA: DECA, An Association of Marketing Students, 2005.

Daggett, Willard R. and Gray, Kenneth C. "Educational Rigor & Relevance: An Interview with Willard Daggett" *Techniques* September 2005 Edition. Alexandria, VA: Association for Career and Technical Education, 2005.

DHA. "Business Coalition Leaders Speak Out on Education". Charlotte, NC: DeHavilland Associates, 2007. from www.dehavillandassociates.com

Delaware BPA. *Delaware Association Chapter Management Manual.* Dover, DE: Delaware Association of Business Professionals of America, 2003.

Deloitte Consulting. *2005 Skills Gap Report – A Survey of the American Manufacturing Workforce.* Washington, DC: The National Assoication of Manufacturers, 2005.

Farr, Michael and Shatkin, Laurence. *250 Best Jobs Through Apprenticeships.* Indianapolis, IN: JIST Publishing, 2005.

Future Business Leaders of America-Phi Beta Lambda (FBLA-PBL). *FBLA-PBL Goals.* Retrieved September 22, 2005, from http://www.fbla.org/default.asp?c=100&p=6&featureid=667&menu=104

FCCLA. *FCCLA Chapter Handbook (CDROM).* Reston, VA: Family, Career and Community Leaders of America, 2004.

FFA. *2005-2006 Official Manual.* Indianapolis, IN: National FFA, 2005.

Finch, Curtis R. and Crunkilton, John R. *Curriculum Development in Vocational and Technical Education.* Boston, MA: Allyn and Bacon, Fourth Edition, 1993.

Finch, Curtis R. and McGough, Robert L. *Administering and Supervising Occupational Education.* Prospect Heights, IL: Waveland Press, Inc., 1982.

Fong, Michael; Goodwin, David; Silverberg, Marsha; and Warner, Elizabeth. *National Assessment of Vocational Education: Final Report to Congress.* Washington, DC: U.S. Department of Education, 2004.

Giachino, Joseph W. and Gallington, Ralph O. *Course Construction in Industrial Arts, Vocational and Technical Education.* Homewood, IL: American Technical Publishers, Inc., Fourth Edition, 1977.

Gladieux, Lawrence and Perna, Laura. *Borrowers Who Drop Out: A Neglected Aspect of the College Student Loan Trend.* San Jose, CA: The National Center for Public Policy and Higher Education, 2005.

Goldhammer, Robert; Anderson, Robert H.; and Krajewski, Robert J. *Clinical Supervision: Special Methods For The Supervision of Teachers.* Orlando, FL: Harcourt Brace Jovanovich College Publishers, 3rd Edition, 1993.

Goleman, Daniel. *Emotional Intelligence: Why it can matter more than IQ.* New York, NY: Bantam Books, 1995.

Gordon, Edward E. *Skill Wars: Winning the Battle for Productivity and Profit.* Boston, MA: Butterworth-Heinmann, 2000.

Gray, Kenneth C. and Herr, Edwin L. *Workforce Education: The Basics.* Needham Heights, MA: Allyn & Bacon, 1998.

Gray, Kenneth "High School Vocational Education: Facing an Uncertain Future", *Vocational Education in the 1990s: Major Issues.* Albert J. Paulter, Jr. Editor. Ann Arbor, MI: Prakken Publications, Inc., 1990.

Dale R. Derrickson, Ed.D.

Grubb, W. Norton; Badway, Norena: Bell, Denise; Chi, Bernadette; King, Chris; Herr, Julie; Prince, Heath; Kazis, Richard; Hicks, Lisa; and Taylor, Judith Combes. *Toward Order from Chaos: State Efforts to Reform Workforce Development Systems.* Berkley, CA: National Center for Research in Vocational Education, 1999.

Heacox, Diane. *Differentiating Instruction in the Regular Classroom.* Minneapolis, MN: Free Spirit Publishing, 2002.

Health Occupations Students of America. *HOSA Handbook: Section A, National HOSA – The Organization.* Flower Mound, TX: HOSA, 2004 Edition.

Herman, Roger; Gioia, Joyce; and Olivo, Tom. *Impending Crisis: Too Many Jobs - Too Few People.* Winchester, VA: Oakhill Press, 2003.

Hoffman, Charlene M. *Federal Support for Education: Fiscal Years 1980 to 2000.* Washington, DC: U.S. Department of Education, National Center for Education Statistics, 2000.

Hogg, Cheryl L. "Vocational Education: Past, Present, and Future", *Workforce Education: Issues for the New Century.* Albert J. Paulter, Jr, Editor. Ann Arbor, MI: Prakken Publications, Inc., 1999.

Hudson, Lisa. "The Data on Vocational Education (DOVE) System", *Education Statistics Quarterly*, Volume 2, Issue 4, National Center for Education Statistics, February 23, 2001. http://nces.ed.gov/programs/quarterly/vol_2/2_4/f_section1.asp

Hull, Dan. *Career Pathways: Education with a purpose.* Waco, TX: CORD Communications, 2005.

ITEA. *Advancing Excellence in Technological Literacy: Student Assessment, Professional Development, and Program Standards.* Reston, VA: International Technology Education Association (ITEA), 2003.

Kagan, Jerome and Segal, Julius. *Psychology: An Introduction.* Orlando, FL: Harcourt Brace Jovanovich, Publishers, 6th Edition, 1988.

Kemple, James J.. *Career Academies: Impacts on Students' Initial Transitions to Post-secondary Education and Employment.* New York, NY: Manpower Demonstration Research Corporation, 2001.

Larsen, Luke J. *The Foreign-Born Population in the United States: 2003.* Current Population Reports, P20-551, Washington, DC: U.S. Census bureau, 2004.

Lawrence, Tim. "Welcome from SkillsUSA" *Medallion: SkillsUSA's Official Conference Magazine.* Liberty, MO: Banta Publications Group, 2005.

Lee, Linda. *Success without College.* New York, NY: Doubleday, 2000.

Littrell, J.J.; Lorenz, James H.; and Smith, Harry T. *From School to Work: Teacher's Annotated Edition.* Tinley Park, IL: Goodheart-Wilcox, 1996.

Marzano, Robert J.; Pickering, Debra J.; and Pollock, Jane E. *Classroom Instruction that Works.* Alexandria, VA: Association for Supervision and Curriculum Development, 2001.

Mckinney, Kevin. "Immigration Research" Washington, DC: U.S. Census Bureau, http://lehd.dsd.census.gov/led/library/workshops/2003/Workshop2003/ImmigrationResearch2.pdp.

Menacker, Julius. *School Law: Theoretical and Case Perspectives.* Englewood Cliffs, NJ: Prentice-Hall, Inc.,1987.

National Association of Secondary School Principals. *Breaking Ranks II: Strategies for Leading High School Reform.* Reston, VA: NASSP, 2004.

NAVE Independent Advisory Panel. *Earning, Learning and, Choice: Career and Technical Education Works for Students and Employers.* New York, NY: New York State AFL-CIO, 2004.

NASULGC. *NASULGC 2005: People and Programs.* Washington, DC: National Association of State Universities and Land-Grant Colleges, 2005.

National Constitution Center. *Centries of Citizenship: A Constitutional Timeline.* Retrieved August 11, 2005, from http://www.constitutioncenter.org/timeline/html/cw02.html.

National Coordinating Council for Vocational Student Organizations (NCCVSO). *Vocational Student Organizations.* Washington, DC: National Association of State Directors of Vocational Technical Education Consortium, 1990.

National Dropout Prevention Center. *Effective Strategies - Making the Most of Instruction.* Retrieved September 6, 2005, from http://www.dropoutprevention.org/effstrat/effstrat.htm .

National School Boards Association. *Why School Boards? Five Reasons for Local Control of Public Education.* Retrieved August 11, 2005, from http://www.nsba.org/site/doc.asp?TRACKID-&VID=2&CID=199&DID=10887.

NCEE. *Executive Summary Tough Choices OR Tough Times: The Report of the New Commiccion on the Skills of the American Workforce.* Washington, DC: National Center on Education and the Economy, 2007.

NSF Press Release. "Earliest *Homo Sapiens* Fossils Discovered in Ethiopia." Washington, DC: National Science Foundation Office of Legislative and Public Affairs, June 11, 2003. http://www.nsf.gov/od/lpa/news/o3/pr0365.htm.

Perkins IV, *Carl D. Perkins Career and Technical Education Improvement Act of 2006*, Washington, D.C., 109th United States Congress, 1st Session, 2006.

Reardon, Mark and Derner, Seth. *Strategies for Great Teaching.* Chicago, IL: Zephyr Press, 2004.

Rigolosi, Steven A. *Tools for Success: Soft Skills for the Construction Industry.* Upper Saddle River, NJ: Prentice-Hall, Inc., 2001

Scott, John L. and Sarkees-Wircenski, Michelle. *Overview of Career and Technical Education.* Homewood, IL: American Technical Publishers, Inc., Third Edition, 2004.

Seastrom, M.; Hoffman, L; Chapman, C.; and Stillwell, R. *The Averaged Freshman Graduation Rate for Public High Schools From the Common Core of Data: School Years 2001-02 and 2002-03*

Washington, D.C.: U.S. Department of Education, National Center for Education Statistics (NCES 2006-601), 2005.

Shelley, Kristina J. "The future of jobs for college graduates" *Monthly Labor Review.* Vol. 115, No. 7, Washington, DC: Bureau of Labor Statistics, July 1992.

SkillsUSA. *SkillsUSA Leadership Handbook.* Leesburg, VA: SkillsUSA, Inc., Revised 2004.

Stover, Lois T.; Neubert, Gloria A.; and Lawlor, James C. *Creating Interactive Environments In The Secondary School.* Washington, D.C.: National Education Association, 1993.

Smink, Jay and Schargel, Franklin P. *Helping Students Graduate: A Strategic Approach to Dropout Prevention.* Larchmont, NY: EYE ON EDUCATION, 2004.

Successful Practices Network. *10 Key Components of School Improvement.* Retrieved September 8, 2005, from http://www.successfulpractices.org/focus.cfm.

Sullo, Robert A. *The Inspiring Teacher: New Beginnings for the 21st Century.* Annapolis Junction, MD: National Education Association of the United States, 1999.

Techniques Magazine Staff. "An Association is Reborn". *Techniques*, Volume 77, No.2 pg.44-45. Alexandria, VA: Association for Career and Technical Education, February, 2002.

Terenzini, Patrick T.; Cabrera, Alberto F.; and Bernal, Elena M. *Swimming Against the Tide: The Poor in American Higher Education,* Research Report No. 2001-1. New York, NY: The College Board, 2001.

The American Diploma Project Network, *Ready or Not: Creating a High School Diploma That Counts.* Washington, DC: Achieve, Inc., 2004.

The Secretary's Commission on Achieving Necessary Skills (SCANS). *What Work Requires of Schools: A SCANS Report for America 2000.* Washington, DC: U.S. Government Printing Office for the U.S. Department of Labor, 1991.

TSA. National TSA History, Milestones in TSA's History *Technology Student Association Website.* Retrieved July 28, 2005, from http://www.tsaweb.org/content.asp?parentid=406&contentid=413.

TSA, H.S. *The Official TSA Competitive Events Guide: High School Technology Activities.* Reston, VA: Technology Student Association, Fifth Edition, 2004.

U.S. Census Bureau. *United States Census 1990.* www.census.gov

U.S. Census Bureau. *United States Census 2000.* www.census.gov

U.S. Census Bureau. *2005 Table A-1, Years of School Completed by People 25 Years Old and Older, by Age and Sex: Selected Years 1940 to 2004.* www.census.gov

U.S. Department of Commerce. *Educational Attainment in the United States: 2003*, Washington, D.C.: U.S. Department of Commerce, Economics and Statistics Administration, U.S. Census Bureau, June 2004.

U.S. Department of Education, Office of the Undersecretary, Policy and Program Studies Service. *National Assessment of Vocational Education: Final Report to Congress.* Washington, DC: Education Publishing Center, 2004.

U.S. Department of Labor, Bureau of Labor Statistics. *Monthly Labor Review.* Washington, DC: Office of Occupational Statistics and Employment Projections, November, 2001.

Walter, Richard A.. "Development of Vocational Education", *Vocational Education in the 1990s II: A Sourcebook for Strategies, methods, and Materials.* Craig Anderson and Larry C. Rampp, Editors. Ann Arbor, MI: Prakken Publications, Inc., 1993.

Wenrich, Ralph C.; Wenrich, J. William; and Galloway, Joel D. *Administration of Vocational Education.* Homewood, IL: American Technical Publishers, Inc., 1988.

Wiggins, Grant and McTighe, Jay. *Understanding by Design.* Alexandria, VA: Association for Supervision and Curriculum Development, Second Edition, 2005.

Wood, Daniel B. "Suddenly, vocational training back in vogue", *Christian Science Monitor*, October, 12, 2006 Edition.

Dale R. Derrickson, Ed.D.

Appendix

Internet Sites

Business Professionals of America www.bpa.org

DECA, An Association of Marketing Students www.deca.org

Family, Career and Community Leaders of America www.fcclainc.org

Future Business Leaders of America www.fbla-pbl.org

FFA www.ffa.org

Future Business Leaders of America www.fbla-pbl.org

Health Occupations Students of America www.hosa.org

SkillsUSA www.skillsusa.org

Technology Student Association www.tsaweb.org

Made in the USA
Coppell, TX
21 May 2024

32631451R00061